Darren

Up The Arse.

[signature]

CH0074II8I

CLICKBAIT

CLICKBAIT LIFE AS AN ARSENAL FAN

Published by
Legends Publishing

E-mail david@legendspublishing.net
Website www.legendspublishing.net

Copyright 2019

Notice of Rights

All rights reserved. Unless it is part of a published review, no part of this book may be reproduced or transmitted in any form or by any means, electronically or mechanical, including photocopying, recording, or by any other information storage and retrieval system, without prior written permission from the publisher. For information on getting permission for reprints and excerpts, contact Legends Publishing.

All views expressed in this book are the personal opinions of the individuals concerned and not necessarily those of the author, the publisher or the football club. All efforts have been made to ensure the content of this book is historically accurate but if any individual named feels they have been misrepresented your right to reply will be exercised if you so wish.

CONTENTS

FOREWORD

Reading the first drafts of Darren's cynical and brilliant perspective on Arsenal's season was, for me, like walking into my old local pub or tucking into a favourite meal, cooked to perfection.

I say this with a feeling of personal pride and attachment, because about five years ago Darren approached me with the seed of an idea. We knew each other quite well, sharing a pint or two before matches, having originally met, like so many Arsenal fans, through Twitter. (You will appreciate the irony of the medium of our acquaintance as you read on.)

Following my own attempts at writing about my beloved Arsenal and, knowing I had launched a new platform for budding writers called Gunners Town, he asked if he might contribute an article or two. Darren had no real idea if he could write well but his head was exploding with thoughts. As well as that, he'd become disillusioned at what life had become for the modern football fan. The social media circus that dominated was becoming an increasingly divided place and was also rapidly filling with wannabe celebrity fans and the like. He was desperate to have a comical and sarcastic swipe at the expanding and ever more far-fetched world of Arsenal social media, and Gunners Town gave him a supportive home.

The first few blogs were lapped up, initially by those who knew his style and humour from Twitter, but soon by a far wider audience. His sardonic, often harsh, and always hilarious take on the Arsenal week, the worsening media clickbait and the widening extremes in the fan base in the later Wenger era proved the perfect antidote for many of us. There was simply nothing else like Darren's 'Season Diary' column and we were proud he had chosen our website for its home.

Fast forward a few years, the pressures of work and staying fresh and true to himself took its toll and the fabulous columns became less regular. I missed having to edit whilst laughing and changing the strong swear words for milder emphasising adjectives to ensure his work did not fall foul of the aggregators and reached its deserved and appreciative audience. However, as you will have gathered, neither I nor his following need to wait any longer.

The whole of 2018/19 has been catalogued in his inimitable style, so sit back, hold on to your sides and enjoy the ride (complete with sweariness!)

I am guessing to buy the book you need to be broad minded and over 18 but I won't tell anyone if you don't, kids.

Dave Seager

INTRODUCTION

At some point during the last decade or so, there was an explosion in the number of Arsenal related blogs circulating on the internet. I have no idea when it happened, but it was as if I'd woken up one morning to find they had multiplied by a few thousand overnight. There were match previews, match reports, tactical expert bloggers telling us which players should be playing where, in which formation, financial expert bloggers, transfer experts identifying targets around the world, the lot. A blog is a personal thing, though, and it's not for me to sit here judging someone that has spent hours researching and writing, just because it might not be to my taste.

The main problem for me was that it was getting to the point that there were just so many out there that were too similar, all vying for your attention and trying to outdo each other. I decided I wanted to do something that I felt was a little different.

It's long been an ambition, a dream, of mine to write fiction. It still is. What better way to indulge that ambition than to write about the real-life drama that is being an Arsenal supporter? A soap opera where the plot unfolds in front of you day by day, week by week. Heroes, villains, twists and turns, shocks – the life of the football supporter has the lot.

I began writing a "Season Diary", a week-by-week account of the rollercoaster ride of emotions that we Arsenal supporters go through from August to May. The more I wrote, the less I found myself writing about the actual football.

Football is boring compared to the social media saturated, clickbait driven circus that surrounds it, and it was never really my intention to write about the football anyway.

The divided fanbase that came to symbolise the last few years of Arsene Wenger's managerial reign made for plenty of material at first.

A divide that saw thousands of actual grown adults prepared to define themselves and others by acronym; namely the WOB (Wenger Out Brigade), and the AKB (Arsene Knows Best). It makes me cringe just reading that back. It even got to the stage that with the mere mention that you are an Arsenal supporter in the real world, the first question you were asked was "are you Wenger In or Wenger Out then?"

I recall one Saturday, the delivery fella from Tesco clocked my tattoo when I answered the front door and asked me just that.

As difficult as it was to take this question seriously from a bloke holding a twelve pack of Andrex under his arm, my answer, as ever, was "I'm just an Arsenal supporter, mate." (I regret to this day not following that up with "now just give me my fucking toilet roll....")

Writing the diary allowed me to indulge my penchant for fiction for a while, because the more ridiculous it became, the more often the old adage "you couldn't make it up..." sprang to mind. The examples are too numerous to mention here.

However, if I had to pick one moment to sum it all up, it would be during that horrendous performance at West Brom, when a plane bearing a banner with the slogan "No Contract #WengerOut" flew over the Hawthorns before kick-off... followed a short while later by one bearing "In Arsene We Trust #RespectAW." Live on TV. You couldn't make it up. Eventually, however, this became less of a circus and more like a bunch of clowns shouting at each other.

The longer it went on, the more detached I started to feel from something that had long since become completely unrecognisable from the game I fell in love with anyway. A feeling that had been quietly brewing ever since the inception of the Premier League, with football gradually became more of a "product" than a sport.

Football is supposed to be an escape from reality, a chance to lose yourself for a while and forget about the day-to-day stress that real life throws at you.

The big danger is that you can immerse yourself a little too much and lose sight of why you started following football in the first place.

It's a lot easier to fall into that trap nowadays.

We used to have ninety minutes on a Saturday afternoon and maybe a few hours in the pub as an escape, now we have 24/7 social media saturation, and sometimes football is something you want to escape from, rather than escape to!

My own feelings towards football have changed over the last few years, not least this last year, as I have spent the best part of four months off work through depression and anxiety. Getting too involved in the madness that was being an Arsenal supporter, 2017/18, was not the best place for anyone that had merely woken up with the slight hump, let alone anyone that felt depressed. Anyway, in the end, writing about this circus became about as much fun as watching it did, and I knocked it on the head. Everything had become stale – the club, the manager, the team, the fans. The whole damn lot.

The last season in particular had become almost unbearable, summed up perfectly when, as we progressed to the semi-finals of the Europa League, there were some people suggesting that they would rather not win the trophy if it meant the manager staying beyond the end of the season.

That's how bad it had got. Arsène had become such a dividing figure among the fans that the extremes on both "sides" had mutated into something beyond fiction.

The fanbase isn't just limited to match going supporters, and whether we like it or not it's becoming more of a global game all the time. Technology, the internet and social media mean that our world is getting smaller, while our fanbase grows ever larger. The smaller that world is, the quicker the toxicity will spread, and toxicity will, unfortunately, spread more quickly and penetrate deeper than positivity will these days. That's just the way of the world.

Therefore, it was a relief to most Arsenal supporters when the club announced that Arsene would be leaving at the end of the season.

Many still loved and respected the man, but there really wasn't any other answer, as many had also come to resent him.

Twenty-two years is a long time. Arsène had been manager of Arsenal for half of my life, and some fans hadn't even known anything other than Arsenal under Arsène Wenger, so this really was the end of an era. However, whenever an era ends, a new one begins.

As soon as the club announced the appointment of Unai Emery, I felt a change in the dynamic among the fans. My fingers began to itch, and I was ready to pick up my pen again (or rather fire up Microsoft Word again.) It's not just writing about the same thing over and over again any more, everything feels different. I decided to take things a little further and take the plunge into writing the diary in book form.

I write this diary purely from my own perspective. I'm not here to judge anyone that's for sure – I try to be observational rather than judgmental – and I like to think I barely take football seriously enough to offend anyone. Everything you read here is simply the way I see things as the football season unfolds.

What there no doubt will be is delusion, hypocrisy and contradiction. I make no apology for that, as one of the luxuries afforded to the football supporter is the ability to be more delusional, hypocritical and contradictory than in any other walk of life, and think nothing of it (besides in politics, perhaps.)

If we all sat there during a game thinking up carefully constructed sentences so as not to sound deluded, hypocritical or contradictory, things wouldn't quite be the same would they? The chant isn't "we're by far the greatest team the world has ever seen… at the moment, we might be shit again soon though so we'll get back to you next week…"after all.

For that reason, I'll neither dilute nor delete anything. If I say one thing one week and another the next, it's all part of the ride.

There is every chance that in football terms this season will end up being a bit of a non-event, as this is bound to be a transitional period. After spending a number of my forty-four years as an Arsenal supporter witnessing league titles, cup finals, doubles and an unbeaten season, I'm fully aware that my first foray into authorship could end up as "The Season That Arsenal Did Okay But Finished Seventh."

This isn't about the football though, this is about everything that goes with it, and everything that goes with it will be there whether you win the league, get relegated, or have a nondescript, mid-table campaign. We are in transition as supporters too; it's a clean slate and a new beginning.

On a personal note, as the season begins, I am returning to work, so I'm entering a bit of a transitional period myself.

One thing that has stuck with me this year is something my GP said to me when I eventually decided to go and see her; that you can't change anything that has happened, it's what happens next and how you deal with it that you need to focus on.

The next nine months could well be quite a journey one way or another, and it's time for us all to look forward. Hold on tight.

Darren Berry

WHAT IS CLICKBAIT?

Oxford dictionary defines it thusly: "content whose main purpose is to attract attention and encourage visitors to click on a link to a particular web page..." That's a fair enough definition of how it began, but the truth is, it's mutated into something far worse.

Nobody just reports anything, anymore. People barely even speak a closed sentence anymore. Every action is designed to get a reaction. People have been unwittingly tweeting and posting in Clickbait for so long, that the line between the virtual world and the real one has become so blurred, it's led to an inability to distinguish between the two.

The result? People are now actually talking in Clickbait.

That's right; Clickbait has now become a language.

What basically began as a kind of crude sales tactic, has now become a way of life. Nowadays some people just need to be heard, whether they have something to sell or not (although, to be fair, those most fluent in Clickbait do have something to sell.)

Due to the fact that the internet rules the world, hopefully it won't be too long before you can use Google Translate to decipher the bullshit.

Clickbait is everywhere you turn. You can't escape it. (It's in the Oxford dictionary for God's sake!) From the moment you get up in the morning, until the moment you switch off and go to sleep. You know when you switch the telly on in the morning and there's some insufferable bellend giving their opinion on whatever today's bait is? It's the same thing. You can bet your balls that bellend has a twitter account for us gullible fools to hurl abuse at.

It seems that the internet and social media have been the final nail in the coffin for what little, if any, was left of journalistic integrity.

Okay, a lot of people go on twitter and the like to wind people up (not me, guv, I've never done that in my life...) but personally, if I had worked for years to forge a career as a journalist, only to be reduced to spending my days arguing with fifteen year olds on social media, I'd have to ask myself where it all went wrong.

We could be here all day discussing it, so I thought that throughout the book, I would bring you some of the clickbaitiest examples of Clickbait out there, in no particular order (they're all pretty much as bad as one another at the end of the day.) Here's one to get us started....

"Lost and lazy Ozil might have cost Arsenal £42.5m but he isn't worth two-bob... and he's nicking a living"

Neil Ashton – The Daily Mail

It's no secret that Mesut Ozil is a dividing figure among Arsenal fans. Some won't have a bad word said against him and defend and worship him as if he's some kind of cult leader. Others more or less dedicate their Twitter accounts to criticising him to ridiculous levels. This isn't about judging who's better than who in that respect, however.

This is about a "journalist" using the fact that Ozil is such a dividing figure as a classic example of Clickbait.

This article was written after Arsenal went out of the Champions League at Bayern Munich, drawing 1-1 after losing the first leg 2-0.

It bears all the classic clickbait tactics, beginning with the headline, of course. A headline that mentions his price tag prominently, followed by an insult. Cue thousands of Arsenal fans rushing in to abuse Ashton, to be greeted by a swift block. The bullet points under the headline read as follows:

- Mesut Ozil is the highest-paid player Arsenal have ever had
- Midfielder is the most expensive export in German football history
- Ozil was lucky to get to half-time after display in Munich
- He was taken off at the break and replaced by Tomas Rosicky
- Ozil will have scans on a hamstring injury on Wednesday

Buried amongst the insults and criticism in the article itself, there is a short paragraph and a bit mentioning the fact that Ozil suffered a hamstring injury, which I think says it all about Ashton's intentions here (it might well have said it all about Ozil's performance too, but why let something like that get in the way of an enticing headline?)

Five years on, and Neil Ashton is still known as the man that proclaimed Ozil to be "nicking a living", as he is reminded of on a regular basis, along with what else he is known as.

MY NEW ARSENAL WISHLIST

Ladies and gentlemen, boys and girls; welcome to New Arsenal. There is a new manager, a new regime, and a new air of hope for the future. Despite that, we approach the first season of this new era without a great deal of expectation as to what we can achieve football-wise. We are prepared to more or less write the season off and give the new guy a free pass.

Instead of "Victoria Concordia Crescit", we shall adopt the motto "Spes autem princeps, exspectatione sumus humilis" for New Arsenal. This roughly translates as "hopes are high, expectations are low." *

*(I've used Google Translate, so don't shoot the messenger.)

With that in mind, I think we need to adapt our goals for the coming season. Yes, top four and a trophy would be lovely, but perhaps we need to shift the focus a bit. Here are my hopes for New Arsenal, 2018/19, in no particular order of preference: -

Annoy People

I love it when we piss people off. One of the best feelings in football is watching someone like Alan Shearer quietly seethe on Match of the Day, while having to praise us through gritted teeth.

The media, and a number of "pundits", have always loved jumping on Arsenal's back when things go wrong for us.

(This isn't a new thing... if you think it's bad now, take a look at some of the tabloids in the early 80s.) They love it so much, that you can almost see the steam coming out of their ears when things go well for us.

I have no idea why, but Arsenal Football Club's very existence manages to get under some people's skin.

I love that. Always have.

Yes, we slaughter them when they talk absolute nonsense about us, but would we honestly want it any other way?

Basically, however this season turns out, I hope we annoy as many people as possible along the way.

Shithousing

I guess this follows on from the previous item, after all, there is no better way to wind people up with some good old-fashioned shithousing is there? If we can't win anything this year, I hope we can at least take a few out with us on the way. I'm talking proper nasty, horrible stuff here. We've got the type of player that will be up for that now as well.

I want to see Sokratis pulling Dele Alli's pubic hair while Lichtsteiner sticks his finger up his bum. That kind of nastiness. If there isn't some kind of tabloid crusade to have at least one of our players suspended / arrested / deported / hanged, I'll be slightly disappointed.

To go a whole week without a "thing"

I'm asking a lot here, I know. There always has to be a thing with us doesn't there? Win, lose or draw, there's a thing. For example; win a game 59-0 against the team at the bottom of the league, Mesut Ozil scores fifty and sets up the other nine... "shame he can't do that consistently..." Ok, that's a bit extreme, but I'm sure you get my drift.

As I said, I'm not holding out much hope with this one, and I'm sure it won't be long before we find ourselves "debating" over which Arsenal players deserve to be labelled "legends", how much we hate the Puma kits, and a personal favourite - the "who's the better Arsenal fan competition." Cannot wait.

Unai Emery to become a fully-fledged member of Arsenal Twitter

Yes, folks, our new manager has a Twitter account. Okay, I'm sure it's actually manned by his representatives or whatever, but reality is a lot less fun than using your imagination isn't it? I want to see Unai getting involved in the day-to-day circus that is Arsenal Twitter.

I want him to tweet "this is shit", every time we concede a goal.

I want him to tweet multiple laughing face emojis to the official Tottenham Hotspur Twitter account when they lose.

During the transfer window, I want him to reply to every tweet from the official Arsenal Twitter account with "announce *insert name of latest player the club have been tenuously linked with*"

I want to see him reply to every David Ornstein tweet with a meme, or simply "ORNYYYYY!!!!"

I want to see him Photoshop a willy onto Mourinho's head.

I want him to be catfished by someone called @GooneretteHornyTits, who turns out to be a 50-year-old single man living alone in a Kentish Town bedsit. Far-fetched, maybe, but you never know...

Peace in our time... if only for a day

Let's face it, all that WOB / AKB stuff, when you take a step back and look at it, is a bit...well, weird isn't it?

It's not going to magically disappear overnight, but how lovely would it be to go at least a day without Wenger's name being mentioned? For us to view ourselves and others simply as Arsenal Supporters?

You may say I'm a dreamer, but I'm not the only one...

So, there you have it. If we're having the season off as far as the hope of any kind of silverware goes, that's fine, but I don't see why we can't have a little fun along the way.

Anyway... let the season commence!

Week One, August 12th – 18th
A New Era

There could be no better time and place to begin this journey than today, Sunday August 12th, 2019 at The Emirates. The dawning of a new era – The Emery Era.

There is also no better way for this new era to begin than against the current champions, and possibly the best team on the planet right now, Manchester City. A baptism of fire for sure. A measuring stick for where we are now, but more importantly, where we need to be if we are going to be challenging for major honours any time soon.

A quick scroll through Twitter on the morning of the game sees us in good spirits. "En Route to the Emirates… come on Arsenal!" (Or "On route to the Emirates…" if you want the grammar police on your case.)

Something that is very noticeable is that there is a new vibe accompanying the usual buzz that greets a new football season.

Arsenal fans are re-energised and looking to the longer-term future now. This is not just the beginning of another season, but also the beginning of a new era.

We have no idea what this new era is going to bring or how long it will take to bring it, and it excites us. It also takes the pressure off somewhat.

If we lose this game, there will be no throwing the towel in, with thoughts of "here we go again…" or "it's going to be a long season… Wenger Out", countered with "… it's just one game… calm down…" and so on.

This is going to be a long ride, yes, but it's one we have only just set out on, rather than one we have been on for years, going around in circles, unable to get off.

Me? I'm writing this while sitting on a sun lounger in beautiful Hammamet, Tunisia. I'm soaking up the last of the sun and dragging the arse out of the all-inclusive beer in the time I've got left here (in Tunisia I mean. I'm flying home tonight, I'm not dying), therefore I will miss the game. By that, I mean completely miss it.

I won't sit here searching for some dodgy stream on the iPad, even if it is offering me links to "single mums that need cock." I won't be following it on Twitter either, which can be quite an experience (usually a rather baffling one).

Well if the manager gets a free pass for the season then I don't see why I shouldn't be allowed to sit this one out.

I will check the score later on, but right now, there's a cold Celtia with my name on it so I'm logging off and heading back to the bar.

Sunday August 12th 2018
Arsenal 0 v Manchester City 2

A two-nil home defeat against the champions. Not a bad result considering recent seasons, and one greeted with a mixture of acceptance and optimism. Acceptance that we are a work in progress, that this journey will take time, and optimism because there were encouraging signs out there today.

It is interesting (and refreshing), the difference in how people have reacted to this result under the new regime and how they no doubt would have under the previous one. Why is that?

Well, it's because this is a new beginning. This is just one game, not just one more game in a long spell. We are a club in transition, but we are also a fan base in transition.

Elsewhere, our old pal Sam Allardyce was quick to stick the knife in on Talksport. Yeah, I'm as shocked as you at that one. I can't bring myself to let this kind of thing wind me up any more, partly because that's what the intention is (a point that will no doubt crop up a lot more in this book), but more so because it's usually bloody hilarious.

"What do Manchester City do? They press, press, press so why do you try and play out when they press, press, press?" "We are getting obsessed with this stupid 'let's play out from the back, split the centre halves either side of the 18-yard box and go and play from there'... it's utter rubbish to play like that all of the time."

Former England manager (ahem) Sam Allardyce there, student of the beautiful game. A man whose own Wikipedia page sounds like it's taking the piss out of him. A man that would seemingly send out his teams – Bolton in particular – to kick the shit out of us and be proud of it too. An early advocate of the "Arsenal don't like it up 'em" attitude that might just have indirectly been the cause of serious injuries to some of our players.

So, onto Chelsea at Stamford Bridge next, and if Manchester City were a measuring stick for what we should aspire to, then perhaps Chelsea are more a measuring stick for where we are now. They are in a similar boat to us and are likely to be more direct rivals for what we are looking to achieve this season while City are no doubt busy winning the league.

Saturday August 18th, 2018
Chelsea 3 Arsenal 2

Another game I missed, then. Not a lot I could do about it either. There was a "keep-my-wife-out-in-the-pub-while-the-kids-organise-a-surprise-birthday-party-at-home" situation going on. A situation that I didn't know about until Friday afternoon (kids are so last-minute these days, aren't they?) I didn't even bother trying to swing it to get to a boozer with the game on. My desperation to watch football hasn't returned to that level just yet.

I did manage to keep an eye on the score though, just in time to see Chelsea had gone 2-0 up, so I went back to my pint, only to return to Twitter just after Iwobi had finished off a brilliant move to draw us level at 2-2.

I walked through my front door (a few minutes before my wife – just to make sure all was ready for the big surprise moment and nothing to do with checking the score, I had lost track of how much of the game was left by then anyway due to the sheer panic over everything going right) to be greeted immediately by the sight of Chelsea going 3-2 up. Telly off. Party time.

The aftermath of the Chelsea game again saw a more optimistic reaction from Arsenal fans. As refreshing as that may be, it is still something I'm having trouble getting used to. It's really weird, man. Where have all the meltdowns gone?!

The general feeling is that we should have been ahead of Chelsea by half time, and we now see this as a positive, whereas this time last year it would have been something very different. Apathy has become optimism.

It can't just be me; anyone that has been following Arsenal for the last few years, particularly on social media, must think this seems a bit weird.

I like it, though. I can't help but wonder how long this honeymoon period will last, which makes writing this all the more interesting.

Week Two, August 20th – 26th
New Arsenal, New Me

I do love an analogy. Therefore, I obviously couldn't resist analogising about the Arsenal fan base after what was a tough beginning to this new era. Picture this; your New Year's Resolution is to give up smoking (again), start going to the gym again (again), and do that "Dry January" thing (what a complete waste of time that is since you then end up spending virtually all of February drunk.)

New Year's Eve at 5pm you jump on Facebook and wish everyone a Happy New Year, early doors, before "you're too drunk to do it later LOL" or "the network goes down" (never happens, does it? If there was any chance of it ever happening, it's more likely to go down at 5pm because of idiots like you isn't it?) and sign off announcing your intentions for the year ahead "NEW YEAR NEW ME!!!! *MOTIVATIONAL EMOJI AND HASHTAG OVERLOAD*"

First day back at work, it's freezing cold and pissing with rain, your train is delayed, you get to your desk an hour late and someone's nicked your chair. Switch on your computer; you've forgotten your password. Which has expired anyway.

"It's okay" you tell yourself, "it's only my first day back, things will get better once I've settled back into things. I will not smoke, I will not drink, and I will take the stairs instead of the lift...." You're not going to let the world break you. Not this time. This time last year, you would be off for four pints, half a packet of B&H and a KFC, at lunchtime. But not this year. This is your year.

That's us right now. We've had the hardest start we could have had, we've lost our opening two games, but still we remain positive. New Arsenal, New Arsenal fans.

The week got off to a great start, with Gary Neville having a lovely little dig at Big Sam on Sky Sports Monday Night Football.

"I saw Sam Allardyce's comments... but Unai Emery is not trying to get eight points from five games to avoid relegation. He's trying to build a team to win the title." Oh, mate. Ouch. He also went on to add this: "In the first year they will be working it out, implementing his ideas and they'll be fifth or sixth. Next year they should be challenging for the top four after three transfer windows. The year after he should be moving up towards first, second or third. My view is this is a three-year project to try and get his ideas into the players."

What he said there is probably spot on and completely in line with our expectations, hence the more relaxed feeling among the fans right now. Hearing it still hit me like a Neville brother tackle on Jose Antonio Reyes, though.

I suppose at heart I'm still one of those that goes into every season with the highest of expectations, even if the head says something different. It is what it is, though. Football tends to move in cycles, always has done.

Bonus points as well to the more intelligent son of Neville Neville for making Jamie Carragher look a complete tit at the same, which admittedly isn't that difficult.

I, and no doubt many others, still feel a little uncomfortable heaping such praise on Neville considering the unbridled hatred we had for the horrible little shit he was as a player, but there is no doubt that he is head and shoulders above any other pundit out there. Possibly ever.

Other than that, there was not much more going on out there, and I attribute this mostly to the fact that we have a home game against West Ham on Saturday that really ought to see us secure our first three points under Emery. Mind you, this is Arsenal, so we will see...

Saturday August 25th
Arsenal 3 West Ham 1

It wouldn't be Arsenal if there wasn't something going on to overshadow the first victory under the new regime would it? So, what is it this time? The price of warm Carlsberg in the ground up to a tenner a pint? The introduction of random cavity searches on Holloway Road? No. Mesut Ozil missed the game through illness.

Cue Twitter sarcasm and insinuation...

"Ozil 'ill' again eh?"

"He gets 'ill' a lot, don't he?"

Ozil has become that bloke at work that rings in sick on Monday, then comes back a couple of days later to such smug, sarky comments as "heavy weekend was it?" and so on.

The fact that people seemed to be talking and tweeting more about this before, during and after the game than the actual football, probably gives you an idea of what the game was like, but three points today was the most important thing and so, the honeymoon period continues for the new manager.

Long may it continue because, if nothing else, it might just give us a break from the childish infighting that has dominated the last few years (I'm not holding my breath on that one mind you.)

As for the game itself, we went 1-0 down, obviously, that is how we do things here. In the end though, goals from Nacho Monreal and sub Danny Welbeck, either side of an own goal, made for a convincing enough scoreline, if not a particularly convincing performance.

Week Three, August 27th – September 2nd
Mesut Özil Ate My Hamster

Three points on the board at the weekend. Our first three points under Unai Emery. The first three points for New Arsenal, and still I think more people are talking about Mesut Özil than the football. It's NEVER about the football any more is it?

If it were about the football, you would never have heard of some of the "journalists" you spend day in, day out losing your nut at on Twitter while they sit there counting the clicks.

The internet is definitely to blame for all of this. If it were not for the internet, there would be no such thing as a click, and therefore no such thing as clickbait for you to respond to.

You could just read the newspaper, wipe your arse with it and move on. Have you ever tried wiping your arse with a smartphone? My advice would be not to. You should probably only wipe it with a newspaper as a last resort, actually.

For those of you that are too young to remember what a newspaper is, it's what we used to read on the toilet before they invented Twitter.

The most important invention of our generation; think of all the things that you wouldn't be able to do without the internet.

Now think about how many people have seen Ian Botham's willy because of the internet.

What could you live without more – getting all your Christmas presents off of Amazon or Ian Botham's chap doing the rounds? Tough call.

(If you're not sure what that Ian Botham stuff is all about, you could try googling it. I should warn you however, that googling "Ian Botham's willy" is probably not a good idea at work. Or in a public place. Or on a full stomach. Or ever.)

Özil's illness soon became "illness" amid rumours of a bust-up with Emery, followed by completely unfounded suggestions that he could be suffering with depression. This is of course a subject that is close to home for me, so I know how delicate a subject it is, and the fact that it's baseless makes it no better than those suggesting he isn't really ill.

Where has this come from? The same place these things always come from – some Twitter person. Here is how it works:

Someone tweets something like "what if Özil's illness is actually depression?"

Someone else sees it and thinks "Oooooh the mental health angle... Hang on, this opinion looks like it might be a popular one soon, think I better sneak on the bandwagon quickly here..."

Then, by lunchtime... BINGO! It becomes an actual "thing" because nobody can be arsed to find out where it came from.

Özil continues to be a polarising figure among Arsenal supporters, and once again, the extremes on both "sides" are ridiculous.

We seem to feel the need for a polarising figure in our lives these days and, with Wenger gone, Özil is among those left behind to take on that burden. Personally, I will be staying on the fence with this one and watching to see how it plays out. Boring, maybe, but better than making a tit of yourself.

One thing is for sure, though – Arsenal fans are clickbait gold, so this kind of situation will always be in the spotlight more than the football. We always have been, but the internet makes it easier, and Arsenal fans are so easy to bait online these days that the media have virtually turned it into a sport.

Thankfully, Monday Night Football provided a welcome distraction from all of that, as our old mate Mourinho continued his now standard third season meltdown with some hilarious behaviour in the press conference following United's 3-0 home drubbing by the homeless Milton Keynes Hotspur.

"Just to finish, do you know what was the result? Three-nil. Do you know what this means?" he ranted, holding up three fingers.

"Three-nil, but it also means three Premierships and I won more alone than the other 19 managers together. Three for me and two for them."

You could almost hear Arsene chuckling from here.

Now, no Arsenal supporter in their right mind ever wants to see Tottenham win – it goes against the grain - but this is the kind of consolation we will begrudgingly accept.

That age-old saying "be kind to everyone on the way up; you'll meet the same people on the way down" was made for someone like "The Special One."

Back to Arsenal-land, and the draw for the group stages of the Europa League saw us drawn in Group E against Sporting Clube de Portugal, Qarabag FK and FC Vorskla Poltava. You can keep your glamour ties against Barcelona, Juventus and the like, playing a team with fewer followers on Twitter than yourself is where it's at. If almost the entire group ain't got a squiggly red line under it when you copy and paste it into Word, is it even real football?

Onto the weekend then, and next up in a series of what should be very winnable games (I know, I know) is Cardiff City away. We have an international break next week, so I have decided to cover the Cardiff game this week in order to have a little waffle next week.

Sunday September 2nd
Cardiff City 2 Arsenal 3

My first full ninety minutes watching New Arsenal saw us facing Cardiff City. Newly promoted Cardiff City, managed by Neil War-nock, who hadn't scored a Premier League goal this season.

If I were a betting man and I had a house, I would bet my house on them breaking their duck in this game. Incidentally, if you bet your house on something, what do you win exactly? Another house? Does the odds system come into play? So, if I were to put my house on Cardiff scoring at odds of, say 2/1, does that mean that I win two more houses? This would get complicated at odds of 15/8, because I would win 1.875 houses, on top of the house that I already own, which is my returned stake.

Then I would have two houses, but also be stuck trying to sell a house with .25 of it missing. Who's going to buy that? "Here we have the toilet, and that hole in the floor is where you poo...." Bearing all this in mind, I can certainly see why it's a bad idea to bet your house on anything.

The major talking points from this game for me were as follows:

Matteo Guendouzi stood out for me early on, and it's clear why he has become a favourite among a lot of fans already. He's full of energy, just as a player with hair like that should be. There is literally no point in having hair like that as a footballer if you're not going to run in a certain way.

After Arsène Wenger having been around for half of my life, it still feels weird seeing Unai Emery as Arsenal manager. Arsène was around for so long, he was like one of the family. Now it's as if I've just found out, after all these years, that Arsène isn't my real dad, and I've just turned up for Sunday lunch to find some other bloke is sitting there at the table in his chair, wearing his suit and eating his potatoes. He seems like a nice guy. I like him, but this is going to take some getting used to.

As much as I like my new Dad, I don't think we will ever have the kind of bond that Lacazette and Aubameyang have. The bromance continues to blossom, so in true HELLO! magazine style, I shall henceforth refer to them as "Lacabameyang."

That little handshake celebration thing they did had me picturing them sitting on a park bench together as an old married couple in fifty years' time, holding hands and reminiscing about the old days with their grandchildren.

As for the football (I really should mention the football), it didn't take long to notice both the differences from, and similarities with, Old Arsenal. The main similarity being that we can't defend for shit and the main difference being the way we try to play the ball out from the back. Unfortunately, Petr Cech..... actually, yeah, just unfortunately Petr Cech. If we are going to continue to play from the back, then from the evidence so far, he at least needs to learn how to do it facing the right way, and passing to Arsenal players.

Still, we are all a work in progress. Oh, and we have an expensive goalkeeper currently getting splinters in his bum on the bench just in case.

We took the lead through a Shkodran Mustafi header from a corner, only for Cardiff to equalise bang on half time.

Lacabamayeng then combined to put us back in front, as man of the match Laca set up, erm, 'Bameyang. Cardiff equalised again before Laca smashed home the winner on 81 minutes.

In summary: great going forward, shit at the back, potential banana skin, might well have lost that last season, three points away from home going into the international break, job done. Bosh. Time for a couple of pints and a Sunday roast. Oh, and that lot up the road lost as well, which is always a bonus.

Week Four, September 3rd – 8th, 2018
The More Things Change, the More They Stay the Same

A break from any Arsenal action this week, the perfect time to sum up the season so far for New Arsenal. Played four, lost two, won two. I don't pay too much attention to the league table this early in the season – in fact I'm not sure what the rules are on when we do start paying attention to it this season - but as it stands, we are in ninth place.

There have been some promising signs as well as some worrying ones, but overall, bearing in mind the start we were landed with, I'm content enough with where we are. That's about it really. We are only four games in, and I think we have a way to go before any in-depth analysis is necessary or even possible.

As ever during an international break, we find ourselves with an Arsenal shaped hole to fill, so what to write about during this break then?

I have always found September a bit of a depressing and irritating month. I'm sure it's not just me either, it's like something you can feel in the air. The summer's coming to an end, kids are back to school, people are no longer either looking forward to their holiday or still chilled after returning from holiday. September is the month when everything returns to normal and people go back to generally being arseholes again. That does feel slightly different for me personally this year, however.

As I write, I've been back at work for just over three weeks, and I'm not really paying a great deal of attention to what month it is. It's day by day, week by week at the moment.

Yesterday I had my fifth session of Cognitive Behavioural Therapy (CBT). For those of you that aren't familiar with it, CBT is "a type of talking treatment which focuses on how your thoughts, beliefs and attitudes affect your feelings and behaviour, and teaches you coping skills for dealing with different problems."

I must say it's had a large impact on me. It's a lot simpler than it sounds too, which has surprised me. I think what's surprised me the most is how the complexity of the mind can be broken down so easily with the right tools. Nothing is phasing me at all at the moment. In fact, there's almost a weird symmetry with the mood around New Arsenal at the moment.

Anyway, that's enough waffle about my mind. Despite the international break, there was Arsenal action of sorts this week.

On Saturday, the Legends Match took place at the Emirates, with Arsenal Legends such as Robert Pires, Anders Limpar, Perry Groves and Jeremie Aliadiere facing a Real Madrid Legends XI.

I didn't attend myself but being local to the stadium I noticed a lot of families with kids in Arsenal shirts in the area, which is always great to see. Of course, none of those kids will ever be able to say that they saw Perry Groves' first game for Arsenal, as I can, but at least they can say they saw Pascal Cygan in the flesh.

That all got me thinking about the differences in going to football when I was a kid to how it is now. For most people of my age, football is almost completely unrecognisable to how it was back then.

I've lived in Islington all my life. I grew up within walking distance of Highbury, and my Secondary School was just five minutes or so down the road from the ground. I remember spending a few lunchtimes there; occasionally buying signed photos of players from the old club shop. I loved that shop. (If you are too young to have seen it, let's just say it was smaller than the one we have at the Emirates now...)

There was something special about getting to the top of Avenell Road and looking down. Of course, the buzz was a bit different on match days, particularly an evening game, but there was this aura around the place that was ever-present. In some ways, that aura was even stronger without thousands of people around. It was a feeling that's hard to put your finger on, but it certainly beat sitting in school eating soggy chips.

I still feel that buzz if I take a stroll down memory lane now. That smell of horseshit, burgers and onions (or should that be horseshit burgers and onions?) is one that will live long in the memories of all of us that were lucky enough to experience it.

One thing I'll certainly not forget, is how less complicated life was at that age, and football reflected that. As a young kid, you went to a football match and you just wanted your team to win. Either all the nonsense around it that there is today didn't exist, or you were just blissfully unaware of it.

You did your arguing about football at school, of course, but that usually involved you insisting the team that you supported were better than the team someone else supported. I went to school when Liverpool were winning the league what seemed like every year, meaning there were quite a few Liverpool "fans" at school.

Therefore, I spent some of the "best days of my life" arguing that Martin Hayes was better than John Barnes. (For the record, for those of you not old enough to remember; he wasn't.)

When I was a kid, everything revolved around football one way or another, from watching it to playing it. Even most of the games we had on the computer were football based.

Fast forward to the current day, and how things have changed (a shiny new 60,000-capacity stadium for starters), and with all the distractions they have, it's an achievement even getting kids to a game these days (not to mention the cost involved for the parents!) Compared to those Highbury days though, everything is shiny and new.

Do those kids look disappointed when they get there? Nope.

Do they sniff the air and wish they could smell horseshit? Not a chance.

The thing is, kids these days, they like shiny and new things. We had Saint & Greavsie and Grandstand; they've been blinded by the bright lights of Sky Sports and "The Premiership", and, as I said earlier, football is as much of a product these days as it is a sport.

I was happy with the smell of horse poop, but I was also happy with a Commodore Vic 20 and a Walkman without a rewind button. I can just imagine the look I would get if I gave either of those to my kids now.

The next generation of fans will not get to experience what we did, but we'll not get to experience what they do now. We had High-bury, we have our memories of Highbury; The Emirates is for them.

Week Five, September 8th – 14th, 2018
Dad, Are We Nearly There Yet?

Football supporters in general aren't exactly known for their patience, and it would seem that an international break has become the ultimate test of what patience we do have left. Well, for the apparently growing number that aren't that thrilled by internationals anyway. It's only one weekend without a game, but by the time it reaches a couple of days into the second week people start to get a bit fidgety and irritable.

I vividly remember sitting in the car on the way to Clacton when I was a kid. Once the thrill of eating at a Little Chef (Google it, kids) had passed, my little brother and I were a pair of impatient, fidgety, irritating little shits, pretty much in my Dad's earhole until we got to that bit at the top of the hill where you could see the sea. "DAAAAADDD.... ARE WE NEARLY THERE YET????" (It is funny how there seemed to be something fascinating and exciting about stopping halfway through a journey to eat at a Little Chef. I suppose our under-developed taste buds had something to do with that.)

That's what's going on right now. Impatient, fidgety, irritating little shits having a three-day long Social Media "debate" over absolute nonsense just because we don't have any football for a few days. So far this season we have been more patient than we have been for a long while as Arsenal supporters but give us a week without a game and here we are sitting in the back of the car whining at the old man. Roll on Saturday.

Saturday, September 15th
Newcastle United 1 Arsenal 2

I remember the corresponding fixture last season very well. Not just because I was watching it in the pub only able to drink lime and soda due to just having begun a course of anti-depressant medication either. Ironically, that was one depressing game.

Some Arsenal fans were going through their "I'm not saying I want Arsenal to lose, but I would rather we didn't win, just in case it means that Wenger will still be here next season" phase.

For me, however much the game has changed over the years, that one thing has never changed since those days of Highbury and horse crap; you go to football wanting to watch your team win a game of football. It's not Wenger playing Newcastle, it is The Arsenal playing Newcastle.

If I ever get to the stage where I don't want Arsenal to win, then I have completely lost what it is that got me into football all those years ago, and I will give it all up. Still, each to their own and all that.

We went 1-0 up in the first half having played some decent stuff, only to lose 2-1. That, however, was then. This is now.

Before the game we had the now standard "why isn't Torreira starting?" questions on Twitter. That is a very good question to be fair; answers on a postcard to Mr U Emery, Emirates Stadium, London N5 please.

Of course, this wouldn't be Arsenal these days if Mesut Özil wasn't mentioned in some way pre-game would it? Turns out that Mesut's 200th game for the Gunners also marks the first time he has started a game at St James' Park. To be perfectly honest, I don't really care.

We took the lead through a superb Granit Xhaka free kick. The aforementioned Özil then celebrated popping his Newcastle away cherry by doubling our lead with a neat finish. Xhaka and Özil scoring in the same game... you could hear the tweets deleted from drafts miles away.

The hosts got a late consolation, which was a bit frustrating, but two away wins on the bounce can't be a bad thing given how few we've seen in 2018. Most importantly, however, we pissed Alan Shearer off, so I can tick that one off on the New Arsenal Wishlist.

"That defeat hurt me more than the City one, or the Tottenham one, or the Chelsea one, because I don't think Arsenal are that good a team," he said, using the tried and tested "if you're own mob are rubbish, bait the Arsenal fans" formula. It's every pundit's go-to thing, probably because we've made it easy for them for so long because of the way we react.

Let's face it, we gave them years' worth of material during the "Wenger Wars" (I'm not sure if that term has been used before, but I'm claiming it for now anyway because it's gold), when any old no-mark could get their fifteen minutes worth out of us, simply by writing an article in the Metro and including their Twitter handle. Okay, those fifteen minutes might have been taken up in the main by being called a "nonce" on Twitter, but that's one of the pitfalls of "fame" these days.

That's now three wins in a row, including two away from home, and the new era is up and running steadily, if not spectacularly. We are now level on points with Homeless Hotspur.

Week Six, September 8th – 14th, 2018
Home Sweet Home

Not a great deal going on out there on the football side of things early in the week. I like that. It's how it should be, and a welcome relief from the last few years where there would be something going on every day, even when there was nothing going on.

Off the pitch came the announcement that Ivan Gazidis is to leave the club and join AC Milan. I probably should give a shit about this one way or another, but the truth is I really do not. I'll leave the ins and outs, pros and cons, Ivan's list of achievements and non-achievements to people that do care enough to bombard your Twitter timeline with twenty-odd tweet salvos about it.

This week sees the first of a run of home games, as Arsenal return to European action in the shape of a Europa League tie against FC Vorskla Poltava at the Emirates. Champions League, Shmampions League; this is proper European football. More importantly, it gives me a chance to get just my second full ninety minutes of the season under my belt from the comfort of my living room, as we enter a period that sees us play four home games in ten days.

OFFICIAL FOOT-BALL TWITTER GOES "FULL FOOTBALL TWITTER"

There's a general theme running through this book about the growing role social media – Twitter in particular – plays in our lives these days. This isn't just the case for us football supporters, of course, it's a part of everyday life in general. It's everywhere. Everything is about Twitter these days.

How many "news" stories these days include something that someone has tweeted? I mean, Donald Trump, leader of the free world seems to spend half of his days dicking around on Twitter. We all do it when we're bored at work, I guess.

Occasionally, I'm unfortunate enough to sit through watching the Piers Morgan Show (I think it's actually called GMB or something, but let's not kid ourselves here) whilst eating breakfast. Yeah, I know, that's enough to put anyone off their scrambled eggs.

If you haven't seen it before; The Piers Morgan Show - let's call it PMS – is basically a vehicle for this odious toad to air his "opinions", occasionally on serious news, occasionally on whatever bollocks they've decided is news today ("should pooing in public toilets be banned? After the break, we'll be speaking to Sadie from Primrose Hill, who's calling for a ban on passing stools in Wetherspoons, after walking into an absolute humdinger on a Monday lunchtime...." that kind of thing.)

Piers then spends the rest of his day quote tweeting Gary Lineker when he inevitably disagrees with him, with them referring to each other as "Tubbs" and "Jugs" for the rest of the day. Honestly, I wish they'd just kiss and get it over with. Apologies, I may have digressed slightly there. It's only a minor digression anyway, more of a setup.

Most Arsenal fans that have Twitter will probably know exactly what you mean if you use the words "Arsenal Twitter." It's like everything has its own Twitter.

The occasions on which these Twitters cross paths can be quite incredible. Any football fan that has had the misfortune of feeling the ire of Cyclist Twitter can attest to that. Man, they are something else. Anyway, Arsenal Twitter also falls under the larger umbrella of Football Twitter, which includes the Twitter of fans of all clubs. Most are as mad as each other, if we're honest.

As much as we love to argue amongst ourselves these days, given the tribal nature of football fandom, there are obviously occasions when we cross Twitter paths with rival clubs. (Stay with me. If you're still here that is.)

Liverpool fans have always been easy to wind up; stick #YNWA in a tweet and they are often all over it in seconds. Mention something about them winning four European Cups and there's every chance you'll have thousands of the fuckers in your mentions correcting you. That's always great for a laugh. I haven't even got started on the #TwitterClarets yet either.

As well as every fanbase having their own Twitter, all clubs of course have an official Twitter account. Some are deadly serious, and generally only there as a source of information (let's be honest, most of us get our information off of social media these days, don't we? Whether it be genuine, useful info or news, or some twat on Facebook telling you that drinking too much Orange juice makes your dick fall off or something.)

Some of them like a bit of banter as well - the official Arsenal account definitely seems quite a bit more "down with the kids" than it used to be. All of this got me to thinking what it would be like if these official club Twitter accounts went full "Football Twitter...."

@SpursOfficial A memorable night as we win our first game in our new stadium! #SpursAreHome

@Arsenal - @SpursOfficial LOOOOOOOL! You got the man from the Go Compare adverts to open your stadium!

@SpursOfficial - @Arsenal How's that gap looking? #MindTheGap #COYS

@Arsenal - @SpursOfficial How's that trophy cabinet looking? #ForeverInOurShadow #FOYS #COYG

@SpursOfficial We've won a European trophy have you?

@Arsenal - @SpursOfficial Fucking hell you lot are worse than @ LFC with their 4 European cups....

@LFC - @Arsenal - @SpursOfficial it's 5 actually #5times

@Robbie9Fowler - @Arsenal - @SpursOfficial *5

@Realaldo474 - @Arsenal - @SpursOfficial *5

@1MickyHazard - @Arsenal - @SpursOfficial - @LFC Typical goons don't even no you're history

@Arsenal - @1MickyHazard - @SpursOfficial - @LFC *know *your *fishing emoji*

@1MickyHazard - @Arsenal - @SpursOfficial - @LFC come back to me when you've won a European trophy #COYS

@Arsenal - @1MickyHazard Nonce

Around 500 Arsenal fans - @1MickyHazard - @Arsenal Nonce

As is the norm with Football Twitter, this would then go on for days until Graham Roberts jumps in and offers the official Arsenal Twitter account out after a couple too many Fosters tops.

The possibilities are endless, and I could literally spend weeks going over the possible scenarios, but I'm sure you get the idea.

It may sound far-fetched, but stranger things have happened, and I live in hope for the day that Official Arsenal Twitter declares that "all cyclists are c***s..."

It will be interesting to see what kind of team Emery puts out for this one. It looks like Emile Smith Rowe and Eddie Nketiah have a chance of seeing some action, and I must say I'm looking forward to getting a better look at the former, who looks an extremely exciting prospect so far.

There has also been the need to restore our double-barrelled quota in the squad, since the recent injury to Ainsley Maitland-Niles followed the departures of Alex Oxlade-Chamberlain and, more recently, FFS-Theo Walcott.

Thursday, September 20th 2019
Arsenal 4 Vorskla Poltava 2

Looking at that scoreline is pissing me off more than it should do. Two daft lapses in concentration leading to two, to be fair, cracking goals from the away side, after we had gone 4-0 up. I think the reason it's so annoying, and this is the general feeling I got from others too, is because those daft lapses in concentration are what have been plaguing us for a while now, and I'm not sure many, if any, of us are confident that they won't just happen at any time. The fact that they happened in a game that really was a doddle makes it a bit worse for me.

The second half was such a doddle, in fact, that it looked like Lacazette was dozing off at one point. Still, I'm not going to sit here and dwell on the scoreline too much. It's happened, the points are in the bag. Job done.

We scored four well-crafted goals too. A brace for Aubamayeng, and one each from Welbeck and Ozil. I particularly enjoyed Ozil's goal, which included a lovely ball from Sokratis, picking out Mkhi-taryan, who went flying over the 'keeper whilst crossing for Ozil to score with a lovely little finish.

Speaking of Sokratis, the common theme among Arsenal fans so far this season is that he has "surprised them." This has been said so many times over the last week or two, that I keep expecting to wake up in the middle of the night to see his face just centimetres from mine, screaming "SURPRIIIIISE!!!!!!" as soon as I open my eyes.

It was great seeing Smith Rowe get on in the second half. I was very impressed by him too. He didn't look overawed in the slightest, put himself about and looked very good on the ball. What made it look all the more impressive was the fact that he appeared to have stepped straight off the set of Hollyoaks onto the pitch. Takes some doing, that.

In all seriousness though, it looks like we have a special one here, and I've not been this excited by a young player since Jack Wilshere. Let's just hope that young ESR's bones aren't made of balsa wood as well. Elsewhere, Alex Iwobi had a very good game, and was probably the best player on the pitch, and I was once again impressed with Guendouzi when he and his hair came on in the second half to join Elenny and his hair.

Unfortunately, this wasn't the hairiest moment of the night (sorry!), as Bernd Leno conceded those two late consolation goals on his full debut. As a side note, Leno also has lovely hair.

Week Seven September 15th – 21st, 2018
There's More to Football, than Football

It's Monday morning. The weekend went too quick. I'm at work. I don't want to be at work. As far as I'm concerned, sitting at work wanting to kick someone in the face on a Monday morning in September is completely normal. I've always thought people that start the week full of energy and motivation are weird anyway.

Thoughts from the weekend; four league wins on the trot, and enough positives in every game now. If you are still looking for negatives then, well, you must be an absolute joy at parties.

The subject that we should be discussing today, though, is whether it's too soon to put the heating on. The answer to this is, of course yes, it is. The heating goes on no earlier than October. Add a layer of clothing if you're feeling it a bit. I actually like today's weather. I'm far happier going out in the morning knowing where I stand, jacket-wise, and hopefully this will be the end of all this needing a jacket in the morning then being too warm by lunchtime malarkey.

Anyway, it's due to warm up later this week and you'll all be moaning that you're sweating your arse off, wishing you'd listened to me and not put that damn heating on. Just a few Monday morning thoughts for you there.

On the football front, there are another two home games this week; Brentford in the Carabao Cup, and a good old traditional Saturday three o'clock kick off league game against Watford. The latter of which, I'm pleased to say, I shall be attending with my stepson, Harry.

The competition originally known as The Football League Cup has seen its reputation diminish over the years. Whatever your thoughts are on that, it is what it is, and with the demands on resources these days, unfortunately something was bound to give.

Some of the sponsors over the years have made it a little harder to take seriously, however. This began back in 1982, when the Football League Cup became the Milk Cup. The youngsters among you may be wondering, as I was back then, how milk can sponsor a cup. It's just milk aint it? The sponsor was actually the Milk Marketing Board, but I guess the "Milk Marketing Board Cup" sounds even worse. It never really got much, if at all, better after that.

Coca Cola was probably the most prestigious sponsor of the competition... Arsenal supporters will remember the '93 final for Tony Adams dropping Steve Morrow after the game - putting him in hospital with a broken arm - after he had scored the winner against Sheffield Wednesday.

There was also our 2007 Carling Cup final against Chelsea, which erupted into a 14-man brawl, with anyone that wasn't piling in like "leave it, Frank, he's not worth it..."

How fitting it was that a cup final sponsored by a piss-weak lager ended up looking like a Friday night in Chelmsford.

Our favourite will obviously be Littlewoods though, as it was the first trophy we won under George Graham. I'll never forget that cup final at Wembley in 1987, the first time I had ever experienced anything like it, and the beginning of a successful period, the likes of which many of us had never experienced.

As well as those, there has been Rumbelows, Worthington and Capital One. The most notable thing that happened with any of those was when the Worthington Cup was known as the "Worthless Cup", not helped much by the fact that this sponsorship coincided with Premier League clubs beginning to field weakened teams.

Following a brief spell without a sponsor, with the competition simply known as the EFL Cup (English Football League, not English as a Foreign Language), we now have the Carabao Cup. Carabao is an energy drink that, according to their website, was "invented in 2002 to help the people of Thailand meet their daily challenges... to be at their best at work and at play."

To sum up, then; over the years we've gone from a sponsor that strengthens the bones with calcium, to one that is more likely to give you heart palpitations and turn your shit a funny colour. That's football mirroring modern life right there.

The fact that the draw for the competition takes place on Quest TV, potentially sandwiched between episodes of such gems as Railroad Australia and Incredible Engineering Blunders, hardly does much for its credibility. I look at the competition in this way now: if we win, great. If we lose, never mind.

Having said all of this, and as much as I've derided the competition somewhat here, I will be fully and shamelessly on board with The Carabao Cup should we reach the final.

Wednesday September 26th 2018
Arsenal 3 Brentford 1

Apart from Danny Welbeck's goals, I didn't see any of this game, so I'll keep this short and sweet. Emery put out quite a strong side for this game, as well as giving starts to a few that are more on the fringe of the first choice XI. It was good to see Welbeck grab a couple of goals, and his second finished off a superb team move. I don't really have much more to say other than we got the job done and are into the next round, and that Bernd Leno does indeed have very nice hair.

I don't feel so bad about the brevity of my coverage of last night's game, however, as the following day nobody was really talking about it once the news that the club had withdrawn a contract offer to Aaron Ramsey had filtered through.

To be honest, the more people are talking about it, speculating about it and bullshitting about it, the quicker it has started to bore me. If I wanted to write a book about things that bore me, I would just fill the book with Aaron's post-match interviews. (Sorry, Aaron!)

I like Ramsey a lot as a player but, ultimately, I will always look at these things in this way; if you don't want to play for The Arsenal, close the door on your way out. Goodbye.

Arsenal are on the verge of a seventh win in a row in all competitions, and that is much more important than one player. There's a good chance that securing that win will make some of this talk go away next week anyway.

Saturday September 29th, 2018
Arsenal 2 Watford 0

The first game I've attended this season. As I've mentioned, these days I don't go to football nearly as much as I used to for one reason or another, and I've also mentioned how much I feel football has changed over the years.

One thing that has not changed however, and one thing you never lose, is that match day feeling. It's a unique feeling, a familiar buzz that can't quite be explained, but one that all football supporters have experienced.

Anyone that has ever attended a football match will know exactly what I'm talking about. The game may have changed, but deep down we haven't. These days it's a global game, and thanks to the internet everyone has their own match day experience as well.

I thought I was starting to lose my appetite for the game quite a bit to be honest. Even with this new era and this new beginning, and even having started writing about it, there was a feeling that deep down something was missing, as if during the last few years I had lost something that I would never get back. I wasn't even that bothered about whether it would come back either.

All it takes is going to a game, however, and it's like it had never gone away. It doesn't really matter what the game is either, and the reason is this; there's more to football than football. That's why I'm writing this book. As I say, it's something that is hard to explain, but the analogist in me can't help but try, so here goes...

It's a bit like Christmas. The build up to Christmas is often better than the day itself. A week or so into December, you start to get in the festive spirit, maybe have a few drinks if you're that way inclined. There's just this feeling in the air, and it lifts the mood. Christmas Day arrives and, well, it can be a bit hit and miss, and sometimes feel like a bit of an anti-climax. My stepson Harry joined me for this game.

Harry is 14, and while talking to someone on Friday it occurred to me that I had been to Wembley twice with my mates by the time I was his age, experiencing the elation of winning a cup final, and the despair of losing one (thank you, Gus Caesar) in the space of a year. I was fortunate enough that we were playing some good stuff and enjoying some success when I first started going on a regular basis in the Eighties, during what was also the beginning of a new era - although the landscape has changed considerably now.

It felt fitting that the first time I've taken Harry to a game, just the two of us, was to be a three o'clock kick off Saturday league game. Bread and butter stuff that I loved at his age (and still love at my age), and something we don't get nearly enough of these days.

After the traditional pre-match pie, it was pub time for few traditional pre-match beers (Coca Cola and Wi-Fi for the boy), then to the ground.

That was our build-up to Christmas done and we were buzzing for the big day. Unfortunately, for large parts of the game it looked as though Father Christmas had left nothing but a great big turd sandwich under the tree for Harry.

I asked him a few times during the game what he thought the score would be, and he gradually went from 2-0 to 1-0 to settling on a turd sandwich and a 0-0 draw during the second half. That wouldn't have mattered one bit though, as we had already had a blinder of a day, why let the football ruin a day out at the football?

Mr Emery had other ideas however, and a couple of inspired substitutions heavily influenced the outcome of the game, as Iwobi and Welbeck set up two late goals in three minutes. The first was an own goal from an Iwobi cross, the second an Özil goal after fine work and a cross from Welbeck. Game over.

I used to love a late winner at Harry's age. I still do. He did too. Christmas Day turned out well in the end.

Week Eight, October 1st – 7th 2018
What If?

After what seemed a busy week last week, it's pretty calm at the moment. The kind of calm that comes with contentment. It's nice. There is still some talk about Aaron Ramsey, but even the furore over that has generally died down. Players come and go all the time, and even though the Ramsey contract situation is ridiculous when you think about it, the more success we have on the pitch, the less people will care. This isn't exactly the first time this has happened, so it's a bit like water off a duck's back for us now.

It looks as though his representatives are doing a bit of spin to make sure the blame falls on the club. That would have had the desired effect this time last year, when Arsenal supporters would blame their tea going cold on Arsene Wenger or Ivan Gazidis if they could, but this is New Arsenal, and New Arsenal supporters are a different animal. This is the kind of contentment that comes from winning games, and surely even the harshest critic can't grumble at a seven-game winning run.

Those seven successive wins have seen us climb to fifth in the table, only four points off the top two of Man City and those perennial media darlings Liverpool. Let's face it, after those first two games you would have bitten my arm off if I'd offered you that.

You will of course always get those that will say "yeah, but we've only beaten such and such..." but, as the saying goes; you can only beat what's in front of you. I think we have a couple of big tests coming for both the team and us fans in our respective transitional periods.

The first will come when we face a "big team", and I suppose that test will come when we face Liverpool in early November. The other test will be how we react to our next defeat, whomever that should come against.

If that defeat should come against Liverpool, do we then react in the same way, with the same level of acceptance, as we did against City and Chelsea in those first two games, or are we expecting (or hoping for) some progress since then? Conversely, should we continue our run of good results up to and including the Liverpool game, do we then start to raise our expectations for what we can achieve this season?

We've been extremely cautious with any optimism so far, but it's only natural for the football supporter to start thinking "what if?" After all, a big part being a football supporter is all about the "what if?" "What if?" makes the FA Cup the greatest cup competition in the world.

"What if?" is exactly what was going through every Arsenal supporters mind during the journey to Anfield in '89 (all nine hundred thousand of them...) Or, on the other side of the coin, what if Henry had put that chance away in the Champions League Final? What if Gus Caesar had never been born?

This is all conjecture, of course, as there is every chance by the time we face Liverpool, everything could've gone tits up, but it's an interesting thing to ponder on while I've got nothing else to do on a Wednesday afternoon.

Amazingly, you occasionally do stumble across the odd (and I mean odd in every sense of the word) person that actively looks for someone that they would have seen as foe during the Wenger Wars to argue with. I can only assume this is borne out of boredom, but if not having something to argue about induces boredom for you, and then you actively go out of your way to look for it, well, that must be bloody exhausting.

I suppose you could put it down to the fact that some people just like to moan and argue with strangers on the internet, if that's your bag, you will always find something or someone to indulge yourself.

It's not that I expected there to be this sudden and complete unity among Arsenal supporters once Wenger had gone, that we would all get together and hold hands in a big circle outside the Emirates, with red and white flowers in our hair and break out into a heart rendering version of "Give Peace a Chance".

That was never going to happen, that was clear before Wenger had even gone anywhere, but it almost seems like the Wenger Wars have caused permanent damage and in some places, it's still going on, with the need for conflict ingrained in people's behaviour.

These days, some people just aren't happy with contentment and harmony, like they can't exist without some kind of conflict or drama in their lives, and it looks to me like that's why some people don't seem to be able to let the Wenger thing go. As I said, it must be bloody exhausting.

Still, I'm not here to judge anyone, let alone alienate half of my potential audience. You might be sitting there reading this thinking to yourself "hang on, mate... I enjoy arguing on social media, so what?" If that's what floats your boat, then all power to you. That's one of the good things about the internet; there's something for everyone!

I would be lying if I said I hadn't done it myself on occasion, a lot of us have. We are all human, and sometimes other humans will do or say something that will get up our nose enough to react to it. Social media has become something of an outlet for that.

None of this is exclusive to Arsenal of course, or even football for that matter, more a reflection of this social media age. I'm only using Arsenal as an example from experience.

At the end of the day, there are literally millions of Arsenal supporters around the world brought together by technology, particularly social media; you're never going to keep everyone happy.

Each to their own and all that, but I would say perhaps it's time to consign the Wenger Wars to history and look forward. As a wise man once said, "life is what happens around you, whilst you are busy pissing about on your phone." Wise words indeed.

Whatever tickles your fancy I suppose, but personally, I would rather look elsewhere for my kicks these days, and that homeless lot up the road are always good for a laugh. The Nomads of N17 (or HA9, or MK1) celebrated what they dubbed a "historic moment" as the pitch was delivered to the building site they're calling their new stadium. I suppose when two of the most historic moments that occurred on their last pitch were The Arsenal winning the league, the bar is set pretty low for them.

Thursday October 4th
Qarabag FK 0 Arsenal 3

A trip to Baku, Azerbaijan to face Qarabag FK, managed by the brilliantly named Gurban Gurbanov, the best name I've heard since Boaty McBoatface.

The only thing we needed to do here was win the game. Emery made a number of changes, including going with three at the back. With the way we are defending, and still managing to keep consecutive clean sheets, I'm wondering if he's thinking of just taking one defender away each game and seeing how that goes.

It was one of those defenders, Sokratis, who got us off to the perfect start, scoring his first goal for the club after just four minutes.

Young Smith Rowe doubled the tally in the second half with his first senior goal, before Guendouzi also opened his Arsenal account when he added the third.

Three different goal scorers, all with their first goals for Arsenal. Excellent. This wasn't as comfortable as the scoreline suggests, however, and we had to dig deep for parts of the game. In the end though, it's another win for us and keeps the momentum going.

Week Nine, October 7th – 14th 2018
War is over... We're Getting Our Arsenal Back

I'm generally an outwardly positive person, even during times when deep down I'm not so much. In football terms, that means I go into every game thinking we can win it. I reckon that if we were playing Barcelona with so many injuries that Emery had to send Steve Bould round the boozers on Blackstock Road looking for someone to play centre half with him; you would still hear me saying, "Well, if we can nick an early goal...."

However, and I hate to use this old cliché again, I think this game might be a potential banana skin. Geoff.

An early kick off, away from home, after a trip to Azerbaijan on Thursday. A midday kick-off is as early as it can get as well. It's not far off playing at Hackney Marshes on a Sunday morning. Let's hope someone doesn't get hit really hard in the thigh with the ball during the warm up eh? Stings like a bastard, does that.

Let's also hope that none of our players turn up more or less straight from the pub, still pissed from Saturday night, with a knee injury caused by being thrown down the stairs by some bouncers, like someone I know did over the marshes one Sunday, many moons ago....

Deep down, I have a bad feeling about this game. I said last week, that our next defeat will be a test for us fans as well as the team. I'm not even sure how I will react to our next defeat myself. In recent years, I've been able to brush most of them off quite easily. Losing certainly didn't matter to me as much as it used to.

Some of that has come with age I think, and having a lot more going on in real life these days, but as well as that, I'd had enough of the childish bickering that seemed to follow every defeat. I really don't have time for people flinging virtual shit at each other for hours and days after a game of football.

We are generally more unified as a fanbase right now, however, it will be interesting to see how we react to defeat. I'm enjoying this winning run, my enthusiasm is returning more game by game, and I personally do not want it to be ended by Fulham, thank you very much. Anyway, just a few pre-match Sunday thoughts for you there while I clean my kitchen windows. Onto the game....

Sunday October 7th 2018
Fulham 1 Arsenal 5

For no reason in particular (possibly because I have no beer), I thought I would write about this game sort-of-live. I'm no Brian Moore though, so don't expect too much. The team selection hasn't really done anything to ease my worries about this game, with Özil ringing in sick again, this time with a bad back (you've done that before, don't lie.) Welbeck joins Laca up top, as his other half 'Bamayeng has apparently been suffering with a case of the two-bob bits recently, and drops to the bench, so to speak.

First Half... Fulham haven't started too badly, but we are starting to create a few chances, with Iwobi in particular causing some problems down their right-hand side. Torreira is looking very good as well. Lacazette opens the scoring after more good work down that side, this time Monreal providing the final ball, and Laca turning and finishing superbly. One-Nil to The Arsenal. Get in.

We are starting to play some good stuff now. Of course, recent experience tells me not to get too carried away, because if I had a pound for every time we've played well in the first half, not scored another goal, and everything has gone pear-shaped, I'd probably have quite a few quid by now. Today though, I feel a bit differently, I'm not expecting things to go pear-shaped. I'm not sure why that is, and I don't really care. The sun is shining, the Arsenal fans are in great voice, we're all enjoying the moment. It looks like the team are feeling it too.

And... there you go. The up-and-down-rollercoaster life of the Arsenal fan encapsulated in five minutes right there, as Fulham equalise just as I'm getting carried away with myself. I'm all up for our new playing out from the back thing, but there is a time and place for it during the ninety minutes, and five minutes from half-time when a goal to the good, is neither. Our second half performances have been match-winning ones a lot lately, however, so let us hope that can continue today. Over to you, Unai...

Second Half... Well, that didn't take long! Four minutes into the second half and Laca scores again to restore our lead. A thumping shot from outside the box, with the Fulham keeper a little slow getting down to it, possibly due to still being slightly erect following a superb save from Bellerin seconds earlier. I don't think the 'keeper is as much to blame as the commentators on BT Sport are though, it was a great finish from Laca, who is in superb form and looking full of confidence.

This has been a great start to the half and the Arsenal supporters are in full voice once more. I still feel that we need a third though because, well, because Arsenal. There's the third, and what a goal it is! A beautiful finish from Ramsey to finish an equally beautiful Arsenal move.

Okay, now I'm getting excited. We may be on a winning run, but this is by far the best we have played during that run, the best we have played in what feels like a long time, and that goal just summed up the confidence starting to run through the team, and the supporters as well.

Arsenal are back, and we know it, as a chant of "we've got our Arsenal back" rings out from the away end. Fulham are deflated and defeated now, and it's all Arsenal. A brace for Aubameyang and it's all over. A 5-1 away win to take us into the international break.

A great result and a great performance. Nine wins on the bounce, and we move into the top four, above that lot and just two points off the top. We may not have played consistently brilliantly during this winning run, we may even have ridden our luck at times, but I think this just shows the effect that picking up results while not playing particularly well can have. To think, as well, that there were people who had a bad feeling before the game eh?

I wouldn't listen to me anyway, to be honest. In the days leading up to a certain game on a Friday night in Liverpool in 1989, I spent a lot of time slating a certain Michael Thomas. In fact, I believe I recall using the words "We have no chance if Thomas is playing..."

or words to that effect anyway. In fairness to me though, he was playing dreadfully at the time, but there's only one thing the history books will remember.

This is one major reason that I tend not to go overboard in my criticism of players any more. I think there might be a few people out there wishing they had followed that lead with Alex Iwobi last season as well now, who once again had a great game.

Monday morning, and a real buzz now accompanies that contented atmosphere. We now have no Arsenal action for a fortnight.

International breaks, as I have mentioned, can be a major pain in the backside from an Arsenal point of view, and this one coming at a time when we really are flying, could really drag. Still, it is good to go into it on a high, and with the confidence that was flowing through the team yesterday, I hope there is less chance of us losing momentum.

With the buzz around the fanbase as well, maybe there is a good chance of us just sitting back and enjoying the break.

The fragile peace following the Wenger Wars, is developing more into a unified fanbase now. Some are still trying to resist it; some even want credit for it, but this is strictly the minority. Tiny voices drowning in a sea of positivity.

"We've Got Our Arsenal Back" may be a slightly premature statement (but an understandable one nonetheless), due to the fragility of this peace, but we are certainly getting our Arsenal back.

The good Monday feeling continues with the popular announcement that Adidas are returning as our kit manufacturer. There is an open goal for them here, if they go "traditional" or "retro" with their first kit. If that happens, we're eventually going to run out of things to argue about (unless it degenerates into one of those "who's the better fan?" competitions that are commonplace on Twitter.) Rebooted bruised banana, anyone?

Week Ten, October 15th - 21st
Thanks for the Emery, it's time to say Hola… Unai's First Day

My first meeting with the players was a very interesting one! I almost got off to the worst possible start as I drove into London Colney. I saw something out of the corner of my eye that almost made me swerve off the road! There was a car coming in behind me, and the driver must have seen what happened because the car screeched to a halt and the driver jumped straight out.

"You alright bruv?!"

I got my second shock of the day when I saw this guy, looking as if he was on his way to a fancy-dress party as Austin Powers younger brother. I was starting to wonder if I was actually in the right place.

"Oh, it's you gaffer!" he exclaimed as I wound down my window.

"Ahh don't worry 'bout that... that was for the last bloke" he chuckled, pointing to the reason for my near miss - a small puppy lying on the ground next to a bush a few feet from the entrance. I now realised it was a stuffed toy, not a real puppy.

I sat in my car for a moment to compose myself, wondering what had just happened, as the other guy drove past. His hair, tied into a bun on top of his head, bobbed up and down as he went over the speed bumps. I couldn't quite place him. I thought I recognised him from somewhere, but what was that accent?

I shook it off, putting it all down to first day nerves, and made my way in to meet the players for the first time; with the guy I had met earlier entering the room just ahead of me. As I entered, a number of them were huddled together looking at something.

"Hector! You've got to see this one!" someone shouted, waving a mobile phone in the air. "Twitter is it? Ah wot they sayin' now, man?!" my friend from earlier shouted back as he strolled towards them.

"Hector?! But I thought...." I managed to stop myself, as my thoughts suddenly spewed forth, realising whom it was that I had met on my way in.

"Wot boss?" he replied, still looking down at Danny Welbeck's phone "those trousers cost me a fortune, bruv...." He muttered softly, his voice trailing away with eyes still fixed on the phone.

"No, it's nothing." I thought he was Spanish.

The noise died down as the players dispersed from their huddle and started to get themselves seated, filling the chairs from the back row first, until they gradually began to join a young man who had already been sat in the centre chair of the front row since before I had walked in. He was wearing an Arsenal scarf over his club blazer, which had an Arsenal rosette pinned to the lapel. I recognised him straight away as Carl Jenkinson.

In the corner, I spotted Aubameyang and Lacazette; it looked like they were practising a little dance of some sort. They stopped when they realised everyone else had sat down, and performed an elaborate handshake - embrace kind of thing, nodded at me affectionately, then took their seats too.

After a brief introduction, I took out my USB stick, powered up my laptop and opened up a number of PowerPoint presentations from the "First Day" subdirectory, inside the main "New Job - Arsenal" directory. It's important to be organised and methodical.

The players were great; very attentive and enthusiastic, and after an hour and a half, I opened up the floor to them.

"Are there any questions?"

As soon as the words had left my lips, a sea of arms greeted me. This could not have pleased me more!

"Yes, Alex?"

I chose Iwobi first, as it looked like his shoulder was going to pop out of its socket, such was his enthusiasm.

"Why ain't you followed me back on Twitter yet, boss?" Came the question. He was deadly serious too.

"Erm..." This threw me a bit, to be honest. I do have a Twitter account but I hardly go on it these days. Twitter's not as much fun as it used to be anyway.

"Sorry, Alex, I haven't had a chance yet. I'll do it later."

Alex gave me a thumbs up as he smiled contently to himself. I looked back into the sea of arms and picked one at random, which turned out to be Mustafi.

"Yes, Skhodran?"

No sooner than the words had left my lips, he was on his feet.

"I've got something to show you!" He looked rather pleased with himself.

"Okay, wha..." This time, I hadn't even finished my question before he came charging at me. His phone, which he was holding in the air, almost came flying from his hand as he clattered into me.

I've seen him do that before. A lot.

"Have you seen my welcome Tweet, boss???"

I stared at the iPhone he had just handed to me, the screen cracked all over. I could just make out what he was showing me.

"Back on top of what?"

He smiled, did a little dance, looking like what I can only explain as a constipated duck, and went back to his chair, straight through the middle of everyone else, most of whom just sat there shaking their heads as if to say "not again..." I thought I would try a new approach next.

"Does anyone have a question that isn't about Twitter?" I asked.

Almost all of the hands dropped in unison, reduced now to just two. "Or Instagram..." I added.

Danny Welbeck put down his hand, leaving just Jenkinson, sitting proudly front and centre with his hand raised.

"Yes, Carl!" I felt a sense of relief knowing he was more likely to ask me something at least remotely football related.

"Did you see my goal against Norwich?" the look on his face was priceless, as he ignored the barrage of groans and paper cups being thrown his way. Eyes wide and full of excitement, he looked like a young child putting a mince pie out for Santa on Christmas Eve.

"No, sorry..." the poor boys face dropped, as if he had woken up to find nothing but an untouched mince pie and an empty stocking.

I couldn't help myself.

"I'm just joking, Carl..." I chuckled, rather pleased with myself, "of course I've seen it!"

I had. I had spent weeks watching videos of all the players into the early hours of the morning, sometimes even past breakfast.

"I can't believe he bantered me off..." Said Carl quietly, his voice trailing off. That was it for the day. An interesting first day to say the least!

Week Eleven, October 21st – 27th 2018
Eleventh Heaven

Arsenal's winning run, topped off with that superb victory at Fulham, has meant that contented feeling has stayed with us. Hence, there wasn't a great deal to write about, and I hate trying to force it. If I do that, I end up making stuff up. (What...You don't think last week's chapter was real? Tsk...)

There is a vibe about Arsenal right now that feels hard to put my finger on, but I'm going to try anyway. When I think about it, it's actually funny talking about the "vibe."

WHEN CLICKBAIT GOES WRONG... ADAM CRAFTON, MESUT OZIL, AND A CUP OF TEA!

O ccasionally, a journalist takes on the might of Football Twitter, and gets a whole lot more than they bargained for. Even from Arsenal Twitter, which is possibly the most reactive entity in the world of football-based social media. That's some achievement. Step forward Adam Crafton of The Daily Mail.

If you don't already know what happened here, allow me to enlighten you... Remember when I spoke about the possibility of Official Arsenal Twitter going Full Arsenal Twitter? Well, on this occasion, that possibility became a reality.

The ridiculous tradition of the "combined XI" was what kicked all this off, with Crafton deciding to choose eleven Tottenham players. Let's have this right from the start; there is no way on earth that anyone with half a clue about football would do that other than for one reason; to wind up Arsenal fans. This hack knew exactly what he was doing.

tl Arsenal FC Retweeted
Arsenal FC @Arsenal · Nov 18
Replying to @AdamCrafton_

GIF

Q 381   tl 6.6K   ♡ 14K   ✉

Arsenal won the game 2-0, and the official Arsenal Twitter momentarily went full Arsenal Twitter and replied to the original tweet with a winking emoji, complete with a GIF of Mesut sipping a cup of tea.

Cue FULL SCALE MEDIA PANDA-BLOODY-MONIUM.

The tweet had originally had a bit of a reaction, but this sent it into overdrive.

(Let's get one thing straight here before I carry on – calling this geezer a dickhead, a nonce or even a c**t is one thing, but vile and discriminatory abuse is something else, something I would never condone, and is never acceptable in any shape or form.)

Of course, as well as Arsenal Twitter getting involved in a big way, Self-Righteous Hypocritical Ponce Journo Twitter had to get involved as well, with the club themselves being blamed for all of the abuse that Crafton got. As I said, some abuse simply cannot be condoned, it doesn't take a rocket scientist to understand that. However, it doesn't take a village idiot to figure out that Crafton and The Daily Mail were looking for a reaction from Arsenal fans in the first place. Want to blame someone? Blame the Daily Fucking Mail, Adam.

49

Pre-Internet and social media, the vibe wasn't something you could feel so much other than on a match day. Now, a vibe is something that is there all the time and reaches worldwide.

It's quite something when you think about it, and that's something we don't do often - think about it - as the internet and social media have become ingrained in our lives. It's one of the reasons, for me anyway, it's been such a drag the last few years.

Well, that as well as underperforming on the pitch of course. No matter what, a vibe will always spread from the pitch outwards, as much as there's such a lot that comes with the football these days; everyone is happier when things are going well out there.

Conversely, when things aren't going well on the pitch, it's almost as if you have to look elsewhere to muster up the enthusiasm for a game.

I think that's easier if you are lucky enough to be a match going supporter. As I've already touched on, there are parts of your match day routine that you will always enjoy, even if that just means taking your mind off of the football!

If you don't have that luxury, you're more likely to look towards the web and social media, and that's where these "vibes" build up. There are millions more around the world that follow Arsenal without being able to attend games – both at home and abroad - and when the online atmosphere is as toxic as it had been the last few years, it can eat away at your enthusiasm.

Unless you enjoy arguing with people on the internet of course, in which case there will always be enough of that to last you a bloody lifetime.

Right now, though, the vibe is just as it should be. On the day of the Leicester game, there is a genuine buzz about tonight. There is excitement, but it's also rather chilled at the same time. It's not like there has been a feeling that we want to just fast-forward to our next game because we need to get back on track or whatever. We seem to have enjoyed this break having gone into it on the back of a nine-game winning run.

The football is shaping our view of Arsenal, rather than the other way around. Even though there is still quite a bit we need to work on, on the pitch, right now we're more like "once we sort out such and such..." rather than "we'll never win the league because of such and such..." the belief is slowly coming back.

It's almost become accepted that we are quite likely to start a game slowly, but I've been impressed that the team don't go to pieces, and we are able to play ourselves into games. We have ridden our luck a few times, maybe, but we've been on the wrong end of lucky enough times to give a hoot about that.

This is starting to transfer to the stadium as well, and the usual groans that exude an air of "for fuck's sake here we go again..." seem less frequent, replaced by a mood of "we'll sort this in the second half, don't worry..." Which brings me nicely onto the next game...

Monday October 22nd 2018
Arsenal 3 Leicester City 1

What was that I said about starting slowly? As sure as eggs is eggs, that's just what happened tonight. We started so slowly that we were almost going backwards, in fact.

Leicester could have had a couple more before they took the lead, especially when Leno saved well from Harry Maguire's massive head.

They should also have had a penalty (which might well have led to a second yellow for Rob Holding to boot) and were generally the better side. Still, we knew it would be okay in the second half, right?

This is New Arsenal. This is Second Half Arsenal FC, not Arsenal FC. Second Half Arsenal are a better side than First Half Arsenal. As it happened, Second Half Arsenal FC turned up once Leicester had gone ahead, led by Captain Özil, who put us level with a delicious finish. There wasn't a player on that pitch who could have finished that the way he did. Beautiful.

It's quite easy to forget that Leicester hit the bar in the second half with the score still at 1-1, as SHAFC produced some truly stunning football after that, with Mesut unplayable.

The skipper was involved again for the second, playing a glorious through ball for Bellerin to put in a cross that left Aubameyang with a tap-in. It was the third goal that was the one though.

If you are an Arsenal supporter, you've seen this goal hundreds of times by now, so I don't really have to talk you through it. If you haven't seen it, hang your head in shame and go and stand in the corner until I tell you to come out.

It started with us playing out from the back and ended with Aubameyang once again finishing from close range following a move that involved Bellerin, Özil and Lacazette. That was football at its most beautiful, from one end to the other.

There was some great stuff after that as well, and we could maybe have had a couple more. Laca will be especially disappointed he left his shooting boots at home. In the end, the final whistle came as a disappointment. We were all enjoying this far too much. Emeryball has arrived.

Mesut was obviously getting many of the plaudits – and deservedly so - but Alex Iwobi's performance was right up there too tonight. He seems to be improving all the time. It's amazing to think of the amount of stick he was getting from his own fans last season. Actually, it's not. These days, people are far too quick to jump on a young player, especially from behind a keyboard. It's not amazing, it's not even surprising; it's annoying. I don't want to bring the mood down just now, though, it's not worth the keystrokes.

There were some great performances throughout, and a special mention to Laca, who managed to do everything apart from score.

So, the winning run continues. Ten wins on the trot in all competitions. Nobody knows how long this will go on for – it's bound to end at some point – but right now, I feel as if Arsenal will win every game until the end of time. I'm going into games actually thinking we will win, rather than pretending that I do, while secretly wondering what sort of calamitous fuck-up we're going to witness this time.

Anyway, we all spent the next few days drooling over the video of that third goal (and sharing it on Facebook), before what could be a tricky Europa League tie at Sporting Lisbon, who have only been beaten at home in Europe in the last couple of years by Barcelona. Add to that the fact that we have never won in Portugal and, yes, this looks like it could be quite a test!

Thursday October 25th
Sporting Lisbon 0 Arsenal 1

We made a number of changes tonight, the most notable being Granit Xhaka playing at left back! He did end up there against Leicester the other night, but I don't think any of us were expecting that tonight.

A bigger worry for me, however, was how long it would be before I threw the TV out of the window, as I switched on BT Sports just in time for kick off (yes, I almost got caught out by the early kick off time) to hear Stewart Robson on commentary.

Once I had heard him tell us at one point in the first half that "question marks were being asked" after our first two games this season, though, I somehow managed to block the Forrest Gump sounding weirdo out.

This really wasn't the best game, quite scrappy and lacking in quality, especially the first half (AGAIN.) You don't need me to remind you about the pattern our games seem to follow at the moment though, and the introduction of Torreira for Elneny in the second half had a marked effect on our play.

Welbeck had a goal harshly disallowed, but not long after, "Dat Guy" seized upon a mistake by their defender after Aubamayeng flicked a pass from Torrerira on, and bang – it was 1-0 to The Arsenal. That seemed to take it out of Sporting, and we sealed our eleventh consecutive win, in week eleven, with that classic scoreline.

Another great week, then. I could certainly get used to this. How impressive was it as well, that our two wins this week have come as a result of some champagne football at home, and digging in for a 1-0 away win in Europe?

Also, whisper it quietly, but I don't think we have played as well as we potentially can yet either.

Get our first half performances sorted, iron out a few defending issues, and who knows?

Just one more thing this week; I'm pretty sure with every week that I'm starting to enjoy this, I'm jinxing us more and more. So, you can probably expect things to start going horribly wrong, very soon.

Week Twelve, October 28th – November 4th, 2018
You Can't Win 'Em All

The longer this winning run goes on for, the more there seems to be riding on the Liverpool game. The next "big game."

Sure, this run may have consisted mainly of games that we should be "expected to win", but they have been games that, in recent seasons, we have "expected to balls up spectacularly."

The media, "pundits" et al are of course doing their best to talk us down at any opportunity. How many times have you seen or heard it mentioned that someone "doesn't see Arsenal as title contenders" in recent weeks?

Paul Merson actually seems to have some weird obsession with trying to convince everyone that we are going to get a hammering soon. I can't be alone in thinking that his comments on Sky regarding the forthcoming Liverpool game a little bit odd.

Merse was one of my favourite Arsenal players growing up, but he's beginning to sound rather bitter now for whatever reason. I think we are all a bit bored with the anti-Arsenal stuff in the media now as well. We're transitioning well as a team and as supporters and as a result, there is more of a togetherness about us now. This kind of thing might have worked this time last year, and got us at each other's throats. Not now. This is how we like it, though. It shows we are doing something right.

It is quite amusing when you think that some of these pundits would be absolutely creaming their little pants had Tottenham or Liverpool gone on an eleven-game winning run. Imagine it...

"So, Liverpool's winning run continues. We'll have the thoughts of Michael Owen and Steve Mcmanaman, as soon as they've finished licking each other..." God, I hate Liverpool. More on them in a bit, though, as we face a trip to Crystal Palace today.

Okay, I know I said this a few weeks ago, before the Fulham game, but I'm really not confident about today's game. I am the opposite of confident. I don't know why, exactly. Perhaps it's simply that the longer this run of W's gets, the more likely it seems to be ruined by a D or an L.

Everyone seems to be worried about Liverpool punishing our current propensity for starting slowly, but if it's going to happen, it could happen anytime.

The clocks went back early this morning, so there is also the worry that we won't start playing until after the final whistle. With all of that in mind, I think I would actually settle for the D today, so to speak.

Sunday October 28th 2018
Crystal Palace 2 Arsenal 2

Well, a D it is then. Better than an L, at least. Of course, there is nothing less satisfying than a good old W on a Sunday afternoon, which we may well have had, were Wilfried Zaha not such a diving little C.

Palace took the lead on the stroke of half time through a penalty, after Mustafi did a Mustafi, and went and Mustafi'd someone. The silly big Mustafi.

You know that "perfect time to score" stuff that people go on about when a team scores just before half time? Well, one of the advantages of Arsenal not getting going until the second half means that rule doesn't apply to scoring against us, so we've no need to listen to people churning out that clichéd load of old pony.

We proved that point when we turned things around just ten minutes after the restart. The equaliser came from an absolute peach of a free kick from Xhaka, and we took the lead when goal-line technology showed that Aubamayeng's effort had crossed the line. Fortunately, there isn't such a thing as handball assist technology, as Lacazette clearly handled the ball onto his best buddy (his shirt was being pulled, mind.) Frankly, I couldn't care less, and neither could you. Palace just got Lacabamayeng'd.

Unfortunately, we couldn't hold onto that lead for our third win in six days, and Palace equalised late on with another penalty.

Laca played a poor pass, Mustafi then Mustafi'd, our makeshift left-back, makeshift left backed, and Zaha went and Zaha'd all over us.

There was contact, yes, but he's thrown himself over Xhaka's leg, in my opinion. Don't give me all that "if there's contact, it's a penalty" nonsense either. Okay, we got away with one in the lead up to our second goal, but that doesn't count in my book. Me, biased? You bet your damned life I am. That's how football works.

There you have it then, our eleven-game winning run becomes a twelve-game unbeaten run. It doesn't sound so bad when you look at it that way does it.

The general feeling over the next few days seems to be a mixture of frustration and acceptance. Overall, a draw was probably a fair result, and it could have been worse for us. Well, so I'm told, anyway; apparently, we would have lost that game last season. Even though we actually won it.

Don't get me wrong, I totally get where that idea is coming from considering our dreadful away form last season, but there will come a point where the line needs to be drawn.

Wednesday October 31st, 2018
Arsenal 2 Blackpool 1

There was also a Carabao Cup game this week, but I saw none of it, unfortunately. We won 2-1 though, with a few firsts occurring; Lichtsteiner's first goal for Arsenal, Guendouzi's first red card for Arsenal, and Carl Jenkinson's first start for Arsenal for... God knows how long. God bless Jenks, out there living my dream.

The draw - probably done on Quest TV during the commercial break on My Favourite Train Toilets UK or something – gave us a quarter final clash at home to that lot up the road. That should liven this competition up for us, and I would now like to announce that I am fully on board with the Carabao Cup again.

There was a bit more Ramsey talk this week, or should I say there was a bit of shit stirring from his representatives on social media. I can only assume that a 15-year old girl is running their Twitter account. Embarrassing.

Have I mentioned that I don't like Liverpool? It's probably an irrational hatred, but then most hatred is irrational isn't it? Especially when it comes to football. Don't get me wrong, it's only Liverpool football club that I can't stand (you have to make yourself clear these days, don't you?) and my dislike for the club goes back a long way. All the way back to my school days, in fact.

As I mentioned a bit earlier, Liverpool were the team to beat back then. It seemed that if you didn't support Arsenal or "that lot", you "supported" Liverpool. Being an Islington boy, I supported Arsenal because I had a connection with Arsenal (despite the fact that my Dad is a Tottenham fan.) Not many (if any) could say they had that same connection with Liverpool; it was just easy to pick the team that were winning things. That bugged me.

I do remember strolling into school wearing my Arsenal scarf the Monday after the Littlewoods Cup Final in '87 though. Monday's don't get any better than that when you're fifteen.

Anyway, I'm a grown up now and I'm over that, but the way the media fawn over Liverpool so ridiculously gets right on my tits. I challenge anyone to sit through a game involving Liverpool that has Michael Owen or Steve Mcmananamanaman involved in commentary and not feel the urge to put their boot through the TV. With that in mind then… onto our next big test!

Saturday November 3rd
Arsenal 1 Liverpool 1

I enjoyed this game. Turns out Merse was wrong. As far as I'm concerned, we came through this test very well. The media have been talking Liverpool up as title contenders this season. They seem to do that every season, in fairness, but after the start they have made, the collective hard-on for them seems even harder. We at least matched them, and overall were probably the better side.

BT Sport decided to put Mcmanamanamanaman on co-commentary for tonight's game – no doubt just to piss me off – and he stated at the end that Liverpool could play better. Bollocks mate. You couldn't play better tonight, because we didn't let you play better.

There were positives all over the pitch once again, and the crowd were superb, possibly because the kick off time meant that a lot of people were, erm, well oiled by the time they got into the stadium.

I sat through this game with the feeling that we are actually a very good side. It's a bit hard to explain, but as much as we've enjoyed some great football these last couple of months or so, seeing us play the way we did tonight against a "big" team, really made me feel that we could be onto something here.

Torreira was superb once again, as was his midfield partner Xhaka. Rob Holding had another great game too, and it's so good to see him getting a run in the side now. Mustafi deserves a mention too – we are all quick to jump on him when he messes up – and he was much better tonight, which is as frustrating as it is pleasing to see, as there's every chance he'll be Mustafi'ing again in his next game. Perhaps he has an evil twin or something.

As much as there were some great individual performances, however, the most important thing is how well we performed as a unit. Once we went a goal down, after what will go down as an error from Leno for me personally, we stuck to it, and a great goal from Laca gave us a well-earned and well-deserved point.

So concludes another busy week of football then, and the transitional period continues to tick along very nicely.

On that note, my own transitional period continues too. Earlier in the week, I had started to feel a few pangs of anxiety. There was no reason for this, other than the fact that The Anxiety Man likes to pipe up and tap me on the shoulder every now and then just to remind me he's still there, like an annoying, attention seeking child.

Satisfyingly though, this also only serves to remind me that I now have the tools to deal with him better, and so The Anxiety Man was dealt with. Do your worst, pal, I got this. Time for a nice quiet Sunday.

Week Thirteen, November 4th – 10th 2018
Squirrels

A few weeks back, I spoke about how we might react to the result of the Liverpool game, both as a team and as fans. I think it's fair to say we've provisionally passed the test as fans, it's now down to the team to show us how they react.

The only thing we are really asking for this season is progress and, personally, I think that this result and performance showed how much progress we have made more than any other game so far.

As for the team, well, it's down to them to show us in the next game, or more the game after the next game really. I have a feeling the Europa League tie at home to Sporting might see a different kind of line-up and, as nice as it would be to pick up the winning thread again, I don't think there will be too much to read into it should we not.

Not really a great deal going on out there at the moment, again showing a sign of overall contentment. No matter how many times I write that word, I'm not sure I'll ever get used to associating it with the Arsenal fanbase.

Thursday November 8th 2018
Arsenal 0 Sporting Clube de Portugal 0

The pavement was a sea of "well-lubricated" green and white hoops, as the Sporting fans drank and sang on the street outside Highbury and Islington station on my way home from work.

The first thing I noticed when the teams came out was that they were not wearing the green and white hooped kit, which had me wondering whether Sporting Clube de Portugal Twitter were up in arms about it.

I often get a feeling from the notes I start making as to what sort of game it's going to be (yes, believe it or not I do make notes during the game.) I've noticed that during the last few games, the notes have started to become predominantly about the football itself, whereas within the first five minutes or so of this one, I had somehow gotten on to squirrels.

Why squirrels? I hear you ask. Well, our old mate Stewart Robson was once again on commentary, and it wasn't long before I found myself wondering if there is anything that annoys me more than Stewart Robson. Turns out the only thing that comes close are squirrels.

Don't trust them, not one bit. Every time I come across one of the little shits, they seem to stop and look at me with those shifty, beady little eyes. I'm sure they're plotting something. They'd have my nuts as soon as look at me, I know it.

Speaking of the commentary, they told us that Unai Emery had apparently been up until 2am studying our opponents, and this has me fearful for our new boss and the potential impact on our season.

Unai being awake and working until the early hours isn't the problem, however, it's more the fact that this was the second time I had heard them mention it this season that worries me. I am now convinced that somebody from BT Sport is spying on him. Your money would have to be on Robson wouldn't it?

Imagine how traumatic it would be for Emery sitting there in his study, compiling his notes on our next opponents, when he gets the feeling that he's being watched. He walks nervously towards the window, slowly draws back the curtains, and sees.... Stewart Robson's stupid fucking face peering in at him. Enough to give anyone nightmares for life, that.

Anyway... the football....

A bit of a defensive crisis saw Carl Jenkinson start the game at left back. You can just imagine the scene in the dressing room before the game, with Emery staring at his laptop, scratching his head...

"What's up, boss?" asks an always eager Jenks.

"We need someone to play at left ba..."

"I'LL DO IT!!!"

"But..."

Those little puppy eyes again... it's easier just to let him start.

Jenks skips off merrily, his little face adorned with an expression akin to the slightly overweight bloke that never gets to start a game on Sunday morning, but always turns up early and helps out with the half time drinks and the magic sponge. His moment comes when he gets to come on in the dying minutes of a friendly, at 9-0 down. He sprints into position just in time to hear the final whistle. Still, he's made it. He shakes the hand of every opponent, then stays behind to take the nets down and takes the kit home to wash it. Carl Jenkinson has an Arsenal bedspread, he can play every week as far as I'm concerned.

Not really a great deal to report on the match, to be honest. This was one of those frustrating, irritating games. In fact, if a squirrel were a football match, it would be one like this.

It was also a match that was sadly overshadowed by a serious injury to Danny Welbeck, who suffered a broken ankle. You could see straight away how serious it was by the reaction of the other players, with Guendouzi looking particularly shaken. I don't think it's unreasonable to suggest that Danny's injury affected the rest of our performance either. A night to forget all round.

You would have to have a heart of stone not to feel sorry for Welbeck. He has had his fair share of bad luck with injuries over the years, and this one has come at a time when he has been playing very well for us.

His contract situation, and likely length of time out of the game with this latest injury, might well mean we won't see him play for Arsenal again.

That would be a cruel end to his Arsenal career. He's a lovely fella, and the good luck messages that were there to be seen in the days following his injury are testament to how popular he is among his fellow pros. Football really is a cruel game sometimes.

Week Fourteen, November 11th – 17th 2018
Remember, Remember, the Crap of November

In recent years, it has been known for us to brace ourselves for the Annual Arsenal November Shitefest from early October, or even checking November's fixtures as soon as they are released, before a ball has even been kicked in anger.

With all the New Arsenal malarkey this season, however, I have only just realised that November seems to have crept up on us. Maybe it's because our form in October took our minds off of it, or that we have a tricky run of fixtures coming in December that's caused us to take our eye off of it a bit, I don't know.

Perhaps our lives are just passing us by quicker by the year and we were blindsided by it. Who knows? Who cares?

In fairness, we have had far worse Novembers than this, and we are still undefeated since we lost at Chelsea, so maybe I'm reading too much into it this year.

Anyway, we are at home to Wolves today and have the chance to break the November hoodoo and go into the international break with a win.

Sunday November 11th
Arsenal 1 Wolves 1

If the Liverpool game showed us what progress we have made since the start of the season, then this one served to remind us of how far we have still to go, both on and off the pitch.

A few things annoyed me about some of the reactions to yesterday's result, and I was starting to feel the need to rant. However, one thing I have learned this year is that anger isn't a good emotion for me to hold onto. I find anger and frustration are emotions that are a lot easier to let come and go nowadays. I'm not saying there's anything wrong with reacting to a result in whatever way you see fit, it's just not for me right now.

Other than our late equaliser, I haven't seen the game, so I'm not going to comment on the match itself.

I went to the pub before the game and met some friends that have books out now, where the special guest was Bob Wilson. What a pleasure it was to meet a genuine Arsenal legend, and what a true gentleman he is. Bob seems to have this aura around him that could be sensed as soon as he walked in, and I honestly felt like inviting him home for Sunday dinner with my wife and children.

I prefer to look upon this game as the day I met Bob Wilson, had a few drinks with some good friends, then went home and cooked a nice roast dinner for the family. Why let the football ruin your good mood? Again, I must stress that this is purely me expressing how I feel about it. If you prefer to look upon it as the game you were proven right about Granit Xhaka or whatever, then you crack on.

The last international break came at a time when we were flying, enjoying our football and generally content as fans. This one is coming at a time when a few games without a win – albeit without a loss too – have us getting a bit tetchy, and some of the old nonsense is starting to resurface. I think we all need a little break from each other, some time to regroup and refocus, and generally just chill the fuck out, frankly.

November isn't over yet, we haven't actually lost a game, but perhaps dropping a few points might give us a reality check as to what our expectations should be. It's only natural to let yourself get a little carried away when you are winning every week, you start to expect to win every week. A little reality check never did anyone any harm. I think the last week is the perfect example of that rollercoaster ride.

One minute we are enjoying the ride and it's all about the football, a couple of games without a win and people are starting to get a bit silly, and we have muppets like that one off of Talksport insulting the entire club and its supporters, enticing us to bite.

As annoying as it can be, it's times like these that are the main reason for me writing this, and serve to show what an absolute circus the modern game is. It can make your head spin a bit if you allow it to.

Arsenal have no game now until the trip to Bournemouth on the 25th, and I think now is a good time for us all to relax a bit and enjoy the break.

Week Fifteen, November 18th – 24th 2018
Arsenal Cliché Bingo, and The Story So Far

No Arsenal until Sunday then, which means that week fifteen, is a completely football-less week. With that being the case, I guess it's as good a time as any to take a look at the performance of some elements of New Arsenal so far. The best place to start is with the manager. I have a lot of time for Unai, and it's great to see the passion he shows on the touchline in Arsène Wenger's suit and tie.

We can't argue with the performance on the pitch at the moment either, as although the winning streak may have come to an end, we are undefeated since losing our opening two games.

While it's clear that Emery is still trying to put his stamp on our playing style, which brings with it the inevitable teething problems, we have played some great stuff at times too. Leicester at home and Fulham away spring to mind.

As far as the new players go, as I said, I was impressed in a few games by Guendouzi, although as much he has impressed me, he is still raw and quite a way from the finished article. This isn't exactly surprising considering that he is just 19, and fresh out of Ligue 2, but I do worry about there being too much pressure on him too soon. Time will tell with him.

The standout signing has to be Torriera, though. He is exactly what we have needed in midfield for a long time, if only to get rid of "Arsenal are crying out for a DM" from Arsenal Cliché Bingo. This is a game created by the media but taken to new heights by the fans, especially as social media continues to take over our lives.

An Arsenal Cliché Bingo card typically consists of other phrases such as "Zonal Marking" and "Defensive Frailties" to name but a couple. Amazingly, "Trophy Drought" is still there too, despite the fact that it should really have moved over to the Spurs and Liverpool versions – alongside such gems as "Made great progress under Pochettino" and "Five European Cups."

Torriera is the first decent "proper DM" we have had since Gilberto (oops, I think that phrase has just replaced the one that we've just got rid of. Still, at least it's a positive one!) Gilberto, of course, wasn't actually known as a "DM", as he was a footballer before a "DM" was a thing.

In the old days, we had things called "midfielders", you see. Now, there isn't a single position on the pitch that isn't abbreviated.

People are even adding bits to positions now just so they can abbreviate them and look smart.

I blame computer games for this. Since when has "ST" been an abbreviation for a striker anyway? That doesn't work. That's just using the first two letters of something, which means it's not an abbreviation, it's sheer laziness. You're pushing it with "GK" for goalkeeper, to be honest. In summary, whoever came up with this idea is a bit of a "CU" if you ask me.

Final mention goes to Sokratis, who is also the type of player that we've needed for a while; a centre half that isn't afraid of a bit of shithousing - a CHTIAOFBOS.

Week Sixteen, November 25th – December 1st
North London is Nervous

Sunday November 25th
Bournemouth 1 Arsenal 2

A nice day by the sea for the fans, but let's be honest, this game is nothing more than a mere distraction before the main event on Sunday. Still, it was good to get back to winning ways after the winning streak came to an end. The elusive half-time lead still, erm, eludes us though, with Bournemouth equalising on the stroke of half-time after we had taken the lead through an own goal. Aubameyang sealed the win on 67 minutes, for Second Half Arsenal FC.

With the team back to winning ways and the first game of the week behind us, there is now only one thing on our minds.

We've had Black Friday (which now lasts until Monday, apparently), we've had Cyber Monday (which is really just an extension of Black Friday, and becomes Cyber Week from Tuesday onwards), we are now on the road to Skidmark Sunday. I am referring, of course, to the upcoming North London Derby.

Let's be honest, none of us enjoy this fixture, do we? For all of the bravado and bluster on display early in the week, deep down we are all well and truly bricking it.

Despite that, this is what we live for as football supporters; the build-up, the tension, the excitement – it's like nothing else, particularly with local derby bragging rights at stake. It's the anticipation of what might come at the end of those ninety minutes that keeps you going. You would have to be some kind of masochist to enjoy it, though.

The only time you can truly enjoy it is if you are a few goals to the good in the dying seconds of the game (even being two goals to the good in the last few minutes can be uncomfortable as we Arsenal fans know very well.)

That's when the relief washes over you, and the release that brings in those few seconds sums up exactly what being a football supporter is all about. If you could bottle that and sell it, you could make a fortune out of it. "Eau de NLD – the unsurpassed aroma of lightly soiled underwear and relief."

It's going to be a long week. You do your best to put on a confident front as much as possible, and you try to find things to take your mind off of it. Keeping your fears to yourself will of course cause the anxiety to build up inside and is, ultimately, the reason that come Friday afternoon you can't concentrate on anything at all as you are a complete nervous wreck. Trust me, I've been there.

Having suffered from anxiety this year to the point that it made me ill, I can honestly tell you that pre-NLD nerves have a similar effect.

Now, I'm in no way trivialising what is an awful condition to suffer from, but I reckon that anyone who has suffered both will know where I'm coming from. The feeling can just appear from nowhere, and washes over you in a split second.

You often feel the need to do anything to get yourself "out of your head", when non-NLD related anxiety comes over you like this, including the compulsion to bury your head in your phone. That is in no way a feasible option this week, as everywhere you turn in the virtual world there is some wally compiling a "Combined North London Derby XI" or something. Whoever invented those needs shooting, by the way. Tim Sherwood, bless him, actually selected a combined XI consisting purely of Tottenham players.

"I didn't worry about Arsenal too much... I tried to look everywhere but I just couldn't find any room for any Arsenal players. I'm not being biased but I just couldn't... Even the most hardened Arsenal fans cannot disagree." Ok, let's ignore the fact that he clearly doesn't understand the meaning of the word "combined" for a minute and break that down, shall we? Of course you didn't, no you didn't, yes you are, and yes we fucking can.

Of course, NLD anxiety isn't as bad as real-life anxiety, because it isn't real-life, but a North London Derby is as close to real-life as football gets. Anyway, let me talk you through the week as I saw it...

Monday

It's there in the back of the mind, but I'm still going over yesterday's performance and getting over a rotten cold, so there is mild distraction. The problem is, that going over yesterday's performance leads to "we are going to need to play better than that against that lot" which leads to "if we don't play better than that against that lot...." which leads to "AAARRRGGGGGHHHHH!!!!!!!" It's going to be a long week...

Tuesday

We find out today that Mike Dean will be the referee on Sunday. They do this on purpose now just to watch Arsenal fans wind themselves up on Twitter, I'm sure of it.

Wednesday

They have a game tonight, playing Inter at their Wembley foster home. They need a win to have any chance of progressing in the Champions League, and you have to think that whichever way that game goes will no doubt determine the mood and the narrative tomorrow.

Thursday

Aaaaaannnnnnd...... they're off! Harry Winks has "warned Arsenal that Tottenham are flying." If my name were Harry Winks, I would be more concerned about how many amusing anagrams can be made from my name than anything else.

I've managed to keep the butterflies at bay up until now, mainly due to being busy, but I know they are there, fluttering away beneath the surface, and Harry Winks is doing his best to stir them up.

We do have a game ourselves tonight, but it's one that is nothing but the slightest of distractions to anyone other than to the Arsenal supporters that have travelled to the arse-end of nowhere to attend it.

Fair play to all of them, I say. I mean, we are all doing our best to put off thinking about Sunday's game, but freezing yourself to the point of having to spend the rest of the week trying to find your genitals (male or female) is taking it to the extreme.

Thursday November 29th, 2019
FC Vorskla 0 Arsenal 3

A comfortable win for the kids and Aaron Ramsey then. Young Smith Rowe opened the scoring early on, and Grandad Aaron doubled that lead with a penalty that he also won himself. A third, a first goal for Young Joe Willock gave us a 3-0 lead at the break, and the score remained that way.

Incidentally, I'm writing this on my phone, and for reasons known only to my phone, autocorrect decided that Young Joe Willock should be capitalised. I like it, and from now on, this is how Young Joe Willock will be known.

Friday

Now that's out of the way, it's time to turn our attention to Sunday. Our attention was always on Sunday really, but at least we could pretend to give a shit about a Europa League dead rubber.

The same way we could pretend we gave a hoot about how that lot and Liverpool got on in the Champions League the night before.

The same way we could pretend to be either amused or outraged about Mourinho throwing water bottles about like a big silly twat the night before that. The same way that we have been pretending that we care about anything else in our lives all week, if we are honest.

Friday 12.39 pm - it's just hit me. I mean, proper hit me. I saw a tweet from the Arsenal Twitter account and it has hit me. Come on Arsenal.

I'm due back at work in twenty minutes; good luck getting anything productive out of me for the next four hours, The Man.

For the rest of the afternoon I've just been knocking about in a state of limbo. Irritable, restless, anxious limbo. A feeling which will now last all weekend, building to a crescendo until kick off, when the adrenaline kicks in and the air turns blue.

Those things earlier in the week that we could pretend to be bothered about are all long gone. I managed to forget about the game for Friday night, with the help of alcohol.

Saturday
The only thing you can do now, is to try and do normal Saturday things. A bit of shopping, a couple of drinks, that kind of thing. We are almost there now.

Week Seventeen Part One, Dec 2nd – 4th 2018
North London is Red

I'm doing this week in two parts, as there is a lot of football to be played this week, including two big games.

Sunday December 2nd
Arsenal 4 Tottenham Hotspur 2

Sometimes, the content writes itself. The whole premise of this book is to capture the rollercoaster ride of emotions that I keep going on about, that we experience during the football season.

Football can take you through pretty much every single emotion there is to feel, and the whole ride can be summed up with that ninety minutes yesterday. The extreme version. If we are talking rollercoasters here, then that ninety minutes was Nemesis Inferno and the football season is the Runaway Mine Train at Chessington World of Adventures.

That image of Eric Dier (you know the one) has become something of a symbol of this game, and I could probably just fill this book with that image on every page. That would be a rubbish book though, and I would be limiting my market to the Dier family, who would probably have given up after a couple of pages themselves.

I don't even have to talk about the game much. I'm sure that every Arsenal supporter in existence has seen it - at least twice – but this week will be about more than the game (again, the whole point of this book. Perhaps I should just give up writing it...)

Okay, so it might only be one game in a long season, and it might only take us ahead of them on goal difference, but today it feels like so much more than that, and today is all that matters right now.

This is the most I've "felt" a game in a long time. There were so many reasons why that I have forgotten a lot of them because this is the type of game that you live every second of. You don't waste it making notes.

That rollercoaster though...

We played some superb stuff in the first twenty minutes, deservedly taking the lead from the spot on ten minutes, after a completely brain-dead handball from Vertonghen. That summed up how rattled we had them. Then that familiar feeling began to creep in, the one that you get when you are dominating a game like this but not extending your lead. It's not a good feeling.

Then followed the familiar feeling that follows that other familiar feeling, like a kick in the nuts, when Dier headed in the equaliser, followed just a few minutes later by Kane putting them ahead from the spot, after someone in the crowd apparently shot Son. It's the kind of kick in the nuts that I've had so often over the years that it had stopped hurting as much, even against them last season if I'm honest.

This did hurt, though. It hurts more now, and it's a good thing. It hurts my sensitive, tender New Arsenal nuts.

Two substitutions at half-time, with Ramsey and Lacazette coming on for Mkhitaryan and Iwobi signalled a change in system, one which paid off when Ramsey fed Aubamayeng, and his fantastic finish left Lloris on his knees.

I was also on my knees in front of the TV when that went in, as I was once more when Laca fired us ahead off of the heels of Dier. Heh, look who's shushing who now, sunshine. The aptly named Dier was then left on his arse as Torreira sealed the win, sending the Emirates – and my front room – wild. Game over. Celebration time.

Time to let all of those pent-up emotions from the last week out. How is the best way to let them out? To take this piss out of that lot.

It didn't take long for that now iconic image of Eric Dier making himself look an absolute string to start doing the rounds. Beautiful.

Three points and we move above them in the table.

It has nothing to do with going above them in the table, though; we play United away on Wednesday, the same night they are at home to Southampton, so there is every chance that we'll only be above them a few days anyway.

No, it's all about the bragging rights. Those beautiful, beautiful bragging rights. Onto Monday we go then...

Monday

Today, North London is red. It's not just North London that's red. Facebook is red, Twitter is red, Eric Dier's stupid face is red. Everything is red, as we bask in the warm red glow of yesterday's result, which ended 4-2 to the team in red.

Tim Sherwood's eyes are no doubt red this morning too, as he wakes up on his living room floor, surrounded by the foul stench of Fosters top and regret.

Whereas immediately after the final whistle yesterday, we were fired up and proclaiming North London's redness to anyone that would listen - and everyone that wouldn't - today we bask gently in the glow of North London's redness. We are totally over celebrating this, and it feels good.

We have won one football match, but we are celebrating as though we have won the Quadruple, World Cup, World Snooker Championship and the Grand National on the same day.

We've earned this. We earned it through spending last week in a constant state of touching cloth. We would be taking the piss out of them if they had been celebrating this way, the same way they are no doubt taking the piss out of us.

How do you react to the insinuation that you are over celebrating? You just stand there and smile. Or, in the virtual world, you post that shot of Eric Dier holding his stupid finger to his stupid lips on his stupid face, time and again.

As I said, there is a good chance they will be back above us in the table after Wednesday's games, which will no doubt lead to them mocking us for celebrating the way we have.

Let them do that, because we were never celebrating moving above them on goal difference. We know. Deep down, they know too.

Also, let's face it, for a club that will probably release a DVD when Harry Kane manages to spell his own name right, in crayon, they're hardly in a position to judge are they?

Week Seventeen Part Two
December 5th – 8th, 2018
The Overcompensating One

As we continue to bask away, it almost slips the mind that we have another big game this week. Manchester United at Old Trafford. I say almost; there is no way the fact we have a chance to beat Spurs and United – Jose Mourinho's United – in the same week would pass any self-respecting Arsenal supporter by.

However, Sunday's result seems to have lifted the pressure a bit. I mean, we are all fully aware of how these things usually go; smash Spurs, spend a few days getting carried away with ourselves... then get beat by a struggling United side.

Again though, this is New Arsenal. New Arsenal haven't been in this position yet, and it would seem that this brings more excitement than it does trepidation.

It's been a different build up to this clash with United; it's been all about Wenger v Mourinho in recent years. I'm surprised Jose hasn't mentioned him yet this week. That's if he can fit him in while talking about himself. I wonder why he does that so often?

In my experience, that kind of thing is a sure sign of insecurity. Surely a man that has referred to himself a number of times as a "champion" is, erm, "overcompensating" somewhat.

The only question here is if the problem is size, functionality or, how can I put this… "over-enthusiasm." I reckon it's a combination of all three.

I can just imagine the post-match interview now…

Arsenal win - "Arsenal beat us, but I still beat Wenger more times than he beat me. This shows that my penis, which I can assure you, is in line with the normal average male penis length, works perfectly well. I have a champion penis."

United win - "I beat Wenger, and now I beat Emery. This proves that my penis is in fine working order and is in line with the normal average male penis length. Bow down to my perfectly adequately sized champion penis in all its fully functioning penile glory!"

I guess bravado is better than honesty in certain situations, and Jose's time in England might well have turned out differently if he had announced himself as "The Floppy One."

Tonight's game is the first time since 1986 that the fixture won't feature either Arsene Wenger or Sir Alex Ferguson. That's some stat when you think about it.

However poor United are in comparison to the United of old, they always seem to be up for it when they play us.

We have only won one of the last 19 in this fixture, which shows they are always up for it, whoever the personnel are, and we all know how much Jose likes a win over us.

This is a big test for New Arsenal. Are we indeed New Arsenal, or just Occasionally Slightly Different to Old Arsenal, Arsenal?

Time to find out!

Wednesday December 5th, 2018
Manchester United 2 Arsenal 2

This was one of those irritating games. You know when you get the feeling it is going to be one of those games straight away? That.

It really doesn't help when it is one of those irritating games when you have Steve Mcmanamanamanaman on commentary either. I know I've gone on about Stewart Robson, but at the end of the day, at least he's just a bitter little weirdo.

Mcmanamanamanaman is a full-on knob.

I have noticed he laughs a lot during commentary, having a bit of "banter" with his pal "Fletch." I'm not surprised he laughs a lot, who can blame him? It's the laugh of a man who is getting paid money to do a job he is clearly very bad at.

Again, I don't like to bang on about the "agenda" or "narrative", but you only have to have a pair of working ears to realise that it does go on, especially on BT Sport it seems.

"Macca's" verdict at the end of the game?

"I know Arsenal are on a twenty-game unbeaten run, but they're not consistent enough…"

Says it all, doesn't it?

They have Phil Dowd on the team as well, as the refereeing expert type bloke. The idea is that he looks at the replays and judges whether the officials have made the correct decision. Now, after United's first equaliser – which cancelled out Mustafi's opener – something happened that summed up the state of both punditry and officiating in this country in one fell swoop.

When asked if Herrera was offside from the free kick that led to the goal, Dowd - while looking at a freeze frame that showed he was offside - conceded that Herrera was "just offside." He then went on to defend the officials, because it was very tight. He then surpassed himself by declaring, "it's a goal for me." Well, if he is offside then it clearly fucking isn't a goal is it, Phillip?

All in all, I guess the fact that we came away from Old Trafford disappointed with a point shows how far we have come already this season. The way we conceded the second goal in particular also shows that there we are still a work in progress, but for me the former outweighs the latter. We are now unbeaten in 20 games in all competitions, which is good going whatever Steve Mcmanaman-amanamanamanaman thinks, and, as I've said a few times already; we all would have taken that after the Chelsea game.

Enough about that, though, as the games are coming quicker than Mourinho this week, allegedly.

Saturday December 8th, 2019
Arsenal 1 Huddersfield Town 0

File this one in the "hard-fought win" column. A lovely late over-head kick from Torreira finally broke down the visitors, but there will no doubt be more "discussion" about the fact that we had three players booked for diving – namely, Mustafi, Xhaka and Guendouzi.

Indeed, Gary Lineker had a bit of fun with it on Match of the Day, reminding us all what an absolute fucking comedian he is by labelling Guendouzi, "Guen-dive-zi."

You don't hear him labelling Tottenham players, do you?

Tell you what, until we hear you referring to "Felly Alli", you can stick to crisps and pooing on the pitch, funny man.

Having three players booked for diving is not good, though, and I'm looking forward to it being next weeks "thing", as much as I'm looking forward to cleaning out the cat tray this afternoon.

Week Eighteen, December 9th – 15th, 2018
It's Oh So Quiet

A relatively quiet start to the week from an Arsenal point of view, especially compared to last week. I am quite surprised that there hasn't been more of a furore over the diving stuff on Saturday, but there are more serious issues being discussed at the moment, especially allegations of racist abuse aimed at Raheem Sterling. Piers Morgan is somehow doing his best to make that all about him, which will come as a surprise to nobody at all. If there had been a big song and dance about the diving bookings, I think we all know what would have happened.

Those people out there that have apparently endless time to kill would be sitting in their bedroom making montage after montage of other players diving and plastering them all over Twitter. This would go on for weeks, if not months until the extremes became so ridiculous that the kind of conspiracy theories surfacing would be enough to make the most hardened flat-earther blush. The media would just sit back, lap it up and count the clicks.

As I write, there is a frankly sickening mass fawning over Pochettino and that lot going on, after they secured their place in the Champions League last sixteen; with just eight points and a negative goal difference, after drawing with Barcelona Reserves, and because Inter Milan couldn't beat PSV at home. I honestly cannot comprehend the love-in for that lot.

Okay, I think we can accept that for the last couple of seasons, they have looked better than they have for a while, but there are actual human beings out there that are more or less suggesting a 1-1 draw with a weakened Barcelona side is the greatest result in their history. I feel sorry for Tony Parkes, to be honest.

I was talking to a friend of mine at the weekend, a Chelsea fan, and we concluded that – aside from the media and Tottenham fans – nobody likes them. That goes for Liverpool as well. We reached this conclusion on only the second pint.

I'm not here to bang on about them though – I've written about them so much lately as it is that I'm not far off disinfecting the laptop with bleach and fire – so I'll leave the journalists to further embarrass themselves by fellating a manager who has – quite literally – not won anything. Ever.

I keep hearing about the "progress" he has made there. Maybe he has, but you get the same trophy for progress as you do for losing eight successive FA Cup semi-finals. On Thursday, we play our final group game in the Europa League.

Thursday December 13th, 2018
Arsenal 1 Qarabag FK 0

A nice little run out for some of the kids and recently wounded, and a result that means our unbeaten run in all competitions reaches the magic number 22, matching the run in George's first season in charge.

Not much to say about the game really, played in front of roughly half a dozen people by the look of it. A nice finish from Lacazette gave us the win, and Laurent Koscielny returned to the side for the first time since that awful Achilles injury, on that awful night at Atletico last season.

A quiet week overall then, a welcome one too, as the countdown to the festive period is now well underway.

We face Southampton away on Sunday, a fixture that hasn't been too kind to us down the years, and with the injuries beginning to stack up, I have a bad feeling about this one. Yes, I know I've said that before, and no this isn't some kind of reverse psychology thing; I really don't feel too good about this one. Anyway, I'll think about that on Sunday. I'm off out now for my annual Christmas jolly up with my wife. There will be steak, there may be alcohol.

Week Nineteen, December 16th – 19th, 2018
Mkhitaryan Helps the Homeless

Another three-game week, another two-parter. The last two-parter was of course the week of the last North London Derby. There seems to be a lot more to talk about when we play them.

Sunday December 16th
Southampton 3 Arsenal 2

Well, unfortunately it turns out that my bad feeling was right, for the first time this season. I'm not going to sit here and say, "I told you so", however. Nobody likes that kind of person. There is a lot of that nowadays isn't there?

"Told you if he went three at the back… blah, blah, blah…."

"Been saying for ages that *insert name of player who has had two bad games on the trot, despite performing well for ten games before that, when this clever dick didn't mention him once* isn't good enough… blah, blah…" Well done, mate, have a biscuit and write a fucking blog about it. Twat.

We all knew this winning run would end at some point, and I think a lot of us could feel this coming recently. The fact that our defence was starting to look like a scene from Saving Private Ryan, bodies dropping all over the shop, meant that it felt almost inevitable. Still, at least someone from Never Wrong Smug Git Arsenal Blog can sit there telling us he knew all along that Koscielny was finished and Iwobi is crap, and this proves him right. After all, winning games and being proved wrong isn't as satisfying as losing and being proved "right" to a smug git.

The game itself? You don't really want to re-live it do you? No, I thought not. If you didn't see it, I will sum it up with the fact that Charlie Austin scored a late winner, from a header. I think that should do it. I think I've lost track of how many defenders are unavailable for one reason or another now, so I fully expect to see Steve Bould turn out against that lot on Wednesday night.

I had almost forgot that we were playing that lot this week, to be honest. It's funny how different the build-up is in comparison to a couple of weeks ago, when it was all that we could focus on all week, whereas this time, it's only really hit me on the day of the game, even though it is actually a cup quarter final.

I guess that one reason for this is that it's the Carabao Cup, and if nothing else it goes to show how far down the list of priorities that is. Don't get me wrong, now that it has hit me, I feel as if this is a life or death game, where the loser forfeits their right to exist as a football club and all of its supporters will be tortured to death, as is the case every time we play them. Nevertheless, you can't tell me it wouldn't have been in the forefront of all of our minds (and our underwear) for a couple of weeks now if it were the FA Cup.

As I've said more times than I care to remember, the biggest test we will face during this unbeaten run isn't actually during the run itself, but how we react when it comes to an end. As far as the team goes, well, that's down to the manager and the players, there is little we can do about that than get behind them as best we can.

For us as supporters, well I think the result of Wednesday's game will have an impact on how we react. Win, and the Southampton game will be forgotten, and we will look at this as the beginning of a new unbeaten run. Lose, and well... I don't really want to think about that right now.

It's a weird one, and one of the reasons it is weird is that I find myself preparing for how to react should we lose. That isn't to say I'm not confident – I'm always confident on the outside – but I can honestly say that if it wasn't against them, I would probably be over losing tonight within a few hours, quarter final or not.

I would love us to win any trophy in Emery's first season (or any other season), and I want us to win every game, it's just that some bother you more than others. Losing to Tottenham always bothers you. A lot. If it doesn't, then you're are doing it all wrong.

Of course, there is always pride and bravado, so I'm sure it will be easy to dismiss this as a meaningless cup that we weren't bothered about anyway. Then of course, on the flipside, should we knock them out, I shall be proclaiming the Carabao Cup as the greatest tournament on earth. Might even buy myself a can of Carabao for a laugh.

If I am completely honest, though, I can't say I'm too confident deep down about tonight. I suppose that is symptomatic of the run coming to an end and our recent form compared to theirs. They've not lost since we beat them and, according to the media, are now the best team that have ever played the game, while our form has dipped worryingly. On to the game then.

Wednesday December 19th, 2018
Arsenal 0 Tottenham Hotspur 2

I'm certainly not going to say I told you so after that. We just weren't good enough tonight, simple. That said, had Mkhitaryan put away the chance he had to put us 1-0 up, we might have seen a different game. He really should have put it away as well. Put through by Ramsey, there was literally only one area of the goal not to aim at, which was exactly where he put it, the tit.

If he scores, they can't rely on the counter, from which they scored both their goals. If my auntie had etc, etc.

I said after that game that it was the most I had "felt" a win in a while, well last night was the first time a loss has hurt me for a while too. Don't get me wrong, they all hurt to a degree, but up until this season kicked in, the apathy had started to outweigh anything else.

I'm taking this as a good sign, a sign of my continuing Arsenal renaissance. You have to take anything good that you can out of these situations, don't you?

Christmas is coming, there is no time to wallow over a football match. At this time of year, thoughts turn to those that are worse off than you are. It can be a particularly difficult time for the unemployed, even more so for those that have lost their job this close to Christmas.

So now that we've done our bit for the homeless and let that lot have their day, let's spare a thought for The Premature One, as he finally checks out of his hotel. I hope he hasn't dismantled his Corby Trouser Press.

While you're out buying Christmas presents, he'll be clearing out the soiled Wenger masks and magazine articles on male impotence from his top drawer. You see? No matter how bad things feel, there's always someone worse off than you.

Week Nineteen, December 16th – 22nd 2018
PART TWO
Where Do We Go Now?

It's virtually impossible to find any positives from any defeat, let alone one that comes at the hands of that lot. Being the positive person that I am (or try to be, at least), I'll give it a go anyway.

That old rollercoaster analogy has really shown itself over the last few weeks. Just 18 days ago, we were all flying. North London was red, the internet was red, and we were positively bathing in it. We were over-celebrating; they were mocking us for it, now they are mocking us a bit more for it, whilst over-celebrating beating Barcelona reserves and knocking us out of the Mickey Mouse Cup (yeah, it's back to being shit again now. Fucking Milk Cup.)

Go back a bit further than that to when we were not even half way through the run, and this idiot here was even starting to wonder whether we could be considered as outsiders for a title challenge. That's how it works though, as I said from the outset; I'll neither delete anything I've written, nor dilute anything that comes into my head, just to make myself look right, because quite often, we turn out to be wrong anyway.

I feel no embarrassment in publishing something that questioned whether we could be considered for a title challenge during a winning run. What is the point in being a football supporter if you can't dream and have a little belief when things are going well?

For us as supporters, I think a reality check might just do us the world of good, because we can now go back even further than that to the very beginning of this new era. None of us were really expecting anything to happen this season.

We expected this to be a transitional season, and we were all pretty chilled and excited at the same time. None of us were expecting a twenty-two-game unbeaten run that's for sure. The new era brought with it a refreshing air, as we embarked on what we knew was going to be a long journey.

The thing is, the longer that run went on, the higher our expectation levels went – however subconscious it may have been – which is only natural. If we can try to settle down a bit and remember those carefree days at the beginning of the season, we will see that we are probably ahead of schedule on the journey due to that unbeaten run, we've just encountered a bit of turbulence along the way.

On a personal level, this is another step forward for me. Six months or so ago, I would not have given much of a toss about them knocking us out of any cup, let alone the Carabao Cup. It might have bugged me momentarily, but that would be it. The thing is, the more I care about a football result, the more I feel that I have made progress from what I was going through mentally earlier this year.

That might not seem to make a lot of sense, but I know what I mean even if nobody else does! There you go; I've just turned losing to Southampton and being knocked out of the cup by Spurs into a reason to be optimistic. Who said depression had to be miserable?!

Saturday December 22nd, 2018
Arsenal 3 Burnley 1

The last game before Christmas often brings with it a party atmosphere. Unfortunately for me, so does the last Friday before Christmas, and I might have overdone it a bit.

It feels like a long time since I attended a game with a hangover. There was a time when I didn't even get them. I hope there is a special place in hell reserved for whoever's idea it was to introduce the 12.30 kick-off.

Ah, Burnley. Home of the #TwitterClarets. What an interesting breed they are. They've never forgiven us for that late Koscielny goal, and we've been living rent-free in their heads ever since. It would appear that nobody has told Sean Dyche and his men about New Arsenal, because Burnley came to be as physical as possible. But New Arsenal don't take that kind of crap any more.

Ashley Barnes was absolutely fuming after the game. I like that, as I alluded to on my New Arsenal Wishlist at the start of the season.

Barnes was fuming during most of the game as well, running around and yapping away like a coked-up Jack Russell.

Two goals from Aubameyang, put us in control before Barnes untwisted his knickers long enough to pull one back.

We made sure of the points in the final minute of the game through sub Iwobi. There was a hint of offside about it as well, which made the boiled Twitter Claret piss even sweeter.

Week 20, December 23rd – 29th 2018
So here it is, Merry Christmas, Everybody's Having Fun

Football is going to take a bit of a backseat for me during the next week or so now. Of course, I will still keep an interest in the festive programme, but my focus will be on the other traditional festive activities. This will mostly involve drinking beer in my pants from 10am onwards (at the latest), and eating until I can barely move.

I have always loved Christmas, but this year for one reason or another I feel the need to embrace every aspect of the festive period. The food and drink. The time with family and friends. The running round like a lunatic on Christmas Eve getting last minute stuff – even though I assured myself that I wasn't going to do that this year (again). The church then the pub on Christmas Eve.

The not being sure what day it is then suddenly realising that it's January and you are back at work tomorrow. Even the cringe-worthy social media posts. Every last drop of it.

There is even a chance that I might get to Christmas Day with-out feeling the urge to murder Mariah Carey. "All I want for Christ-maaaaassss..." SHUT. UP. SHUT. UP. SHUT. FUCKING. UP. Honestly, Brighton could beat us 87-0 on Boxing Day, and I would not bat an eyelid. Liverpool might well actually beat us 87-0 on Saturday and I'll not bat an eyelid at that either. Of course, by then I will have eaten and drunk so much that even batting an eyelid will require some kind of hydraulic lifting device.

Apologies in advance too, as I'm not expecting there to be a great deal of productivity in over the next week or so. Partly because I

"LACAZETTE AND BELLERIN CLASH IN ARSENAL TRAINING – PAIR SEEN SQUAR-ING UP AS TEMPERS FLARE"

THE DAILY EXPRESS

This one is just hilarious. It made me chuckle because it's in the Daily Express. I always thought that was one of those proper newspapers. You know, the ones my parents never bought because they didn't do Bingo cards and that.

"Arsenal team-mates Alexandre Lacazette and Hector Bellerin were involved in a fiery clash during training as tempers flared at London Colney this morning.

The French striker appeared to grab hold of Bellerin after they both challenged for a high ball during a drill.

Héctor Bellerín ✔
@HectorBellerin

It's called banter you click baiters.

MailOnline Sport ✔ @MailSport

Tempers flare in Arsenal training as Alexandre
Lacazette and Hector Bellerin clash dailym.ai/
2HpKWu1

The two players were reportedly swiftly separated, although Arsenal manger Arsene Wenger could do without such distractions as he pursues his final chance of some silverware before stepping down in the summer.

Bellerin has since tweeted about the incident, claiming the coming-together was just "banter""

"Reportedly." By whom, sir? Yeah, thought so.

The funniest part of this were the accompanying photos. Basically, a slideshow that comprised of one of the "bust up", that clearly wasn't a bust up, it didn't even look like they were, erm, busting up! This was followed by three photos of Arsene Wenger with his head in his hands, as if these things were happening concurrently! Honestly, if you haven't seen it yet, look it up. Well worth a couple of minutes of your time to give yourself a laugh. Yeah, I know it's clickbait and looking it up is defeating the object but, let's face it, it's too late now anyway.

feel the need to switch off for a few days, and partly because of the fact that alcohol may play a major part in the festivities. No good idea was ever conceived when alcohol was involved, however good an idea it seemed at the time.

The Spice Girls reunion? You can't tell me that didn't come to fruition during a Prosecco soaked bottomless brunch somewhere. I also have it on good authority that Sir Clive Sinclair was absolutely shitfaced when he invented the Sinclair C5 (Google it, kids.)

Tuesday December 26th 2018
Brighton 1 Arsenal 1

After a nice quiet Christmas Day with the family, we headed off to see friends on Boxing Day, which was of course another excuse for more eating and drinking. As I was unable to watch the game, I followed some of it on Twitter between mouthfuls of Stella and, quite honestly, anything edible I came across. Oh what a joy that was! 'Tis the Season to be Jolly, apparently, but unfortunately nobody told Arsenal that, and our Christmas was ruined. I had a peek back at Twitter a couple of times that evening, only to find that it was now, inevitably, the Season to Be Arguing on The Internet Again. Fa-la-la-la-la-la-la-la-la. What was that about getting our Arsenal back?

For the record, I fully understand anyone getting annoyed with a poor performance and result like that, particularly if you've travelled on Boxing Day. If you haven't already, try alcohol, it's working alright for me.

Saturday December 29th, 2018
Liverpool 5 Arsenal 1

Well, if a draw at Brighton on Boxing Day ruined your Christmas, then this was like Father Christmas coming down your chimney drunk, setting fire to your presents and shitting on your kids heads. Bah, humbug.

Be honest, when you read the, what turned out to be utter crap, I was spouting after we drew with Liverpool at home a couple of months ago, you had a little chuckle to yourself, didn't you? "Title challengers? Yeah alright, wait until he sees what happens at Anfield, the daft twat…" It's all well and good for you, sitting there reading this already knowing how the season finished. I'm writing it not knowing how the week finishes! Still, if you can't laugh at yourself.

We actually took the lead on 11 minutes through Ainsley Maitland-Niles – his first goal for the club – and I was heard uttering that I had a feeling we might get a better result than people were expecting us to. On 16 minutes we were 2-1 down. That, kids, is why you shouldn't drink.

Mind you, alcohol does have its advantages during a game like this, which was 4-1 and all over by half-time. A few people bravely and desperately tried to salvage some pride in questioning the penalty decisions, particularly the first one, but to no avail. The truth is, even if the penalties hadn't been given, we would still have been thrashed. This was the thrashing that Paul Merson had promised would happen, and I am laying the blame fully at his door.

This was the worst we have played in a long time and brought back memories of the kind of thrashings that, at one point, we had almost come to expect. We can be in no doubt now how much work we have in front of us. Enjoy the ride! (Urgh.)

Week 21, December 30th 2018 – January 5th 2019
Forward

So, New Year, new start. Everything has gotten a little serious lately, and I think it is now time to reboot New Arsenal again and relax a bit.

As clichéd as it sounds (I really do hate "New Year, New Me" clichés), the New Year is the perfect time to look ahead, to make plans. Sometimes, however, to move forward it helps to remind yourself where or what you are moving on from, or indeed where you are right now.

Perhaps that hammering up at Anfield came at just the right time in that respect. I guess, then, that this is as good a time as any to look back over the season – and The Emery Era - so far.

We started out on this journey excited, but with few expectations. Happy that we were making a fresh start, and aware that this is going to be a long ride, a process. We lost our first two games, as we probably expected to. We then went on a run of eleven straight wins, including some superb performances, and some fantastic goals, with those against Fulham and Leicester standing out in particular.

The run of wins ground to a halt with a 2-2 draw away to Crystal Palace on October 18th. Despite the end of the winning streak, we remained unbeaten for a total of 22 games – including a 1-1 draw with Liverpool and a delicious 4-2 victory over Spurs at the Emirates – until the 3-2 defeat at Southampton on December 16th brought that run to an end.

Since then, we have been knocked out of the crappy Milk Cup by that lot, beaten Burnley at home, and a disappointing festive period saw us draw at Brighton, and have our New Arsenal arses well and truly handed to us up at Anfield.

Those are the bare facts, and on the face of it, things haven't really been that bad.

There is of course more to where we are as fans than the bare facts, though. Opinions and spin often ruin bare facts, especially in this age of social media, clickbait, and attention seeking morons. There are even people who earn money from ignoring bare facts for the sake of an attention grabbing, piss-boiling headline.

I was reading back over everything I've written so far this season, and it is funny how things change.

There was this thing, which I now know to be some mythical creature that I dreamt up, that I called a "more unified fanbase" when that run of eleven straight wins was in full swing. Let's call this magnificent beast the "Unigooner." A few bad results lately and we are back to the usual moaning and arguing.

The thing is, there isn't really much wrong with either of those things at the end of the day. It's only natural to get carried away a bit when things are going well – that's when football's glorious escapism kicks in – and if that's true, then it's only natural to be pissed off when things aren't going so well. The problem is, as always, we have to take things to the extreme.

I have expressed a few doubts lately regarding the manager, but it's almost always knee-jerk.

Having looked back to the beginning of the season – when I was banging on about how this is going to be a long ride blah, blah, blah – I realise that makes me look a bit of an idiot.

So, am I now going to sit back and enjoy the ride as I said I was going to in the first place? Probably not! I am a hypocrite and I contradict myself on at least a weekly basis. We are allowed to do that as football supporters. I will try though. It's now time for New New Arsenal – #NewYearNewNewArsenal.

On a personal note, I can't say I'll be shedding a tear to say goodbye to the absolute arsehole that has been 2018.

As I have said though, part of moving forward is looking back on what you've left behind you. You can't change any of it, but if it's something you can put behind you, then you can do your best to control where you go, and what you do next. Or at least how you deal with things going forward.

I'm back at work the day after New Year's Day, and I'm less bothered by that than I have been for a good few years.

The fact that I'm not going to have much to do in those first few days, and will spend quite a bit of it sat on my arse, pissing about on the internet is only a minor reason for that too. Honestly.

Anyway, enough about me. The New New Arsenal Era begins today at home to Fulham.

Tuesday January 1st 2019
Arsenal 4 Fulham 1

In keeping with this week's theme of "the bare facts", here are the bare facts... Xhaka opened the scoring on 25 minutes, and that rarest of occurrences that is Arsenal leading at half-time occurred. 1-0 to The Arsenal. We doubled our lead 10 minutes into the second half, when Laca finished off a nice little move involving himself, Iwobi and Kolasinac.

Fulham pulled one back (of course they did) on 70 minutes, before Ramsey restored our two-goal cushion 10 minutes later. The deal was then well and truly sealed by the other half of Lacabameyang a few minutes later.

As far as the reaction goes, it seems it's a case of New Year, New New Arsenal, same old New New Arsenal fans.

When I first started going to football years ago, there was nothing more to a 4-1 win than the fact that you have just scored four goals, and the team you were playing only scored one.

It didn't matter who you were playing, or how many chances they missed. 4-1 was a good result.

I don't remember ever thinking, "If that was against a better team we might have lost." I mean, that just sounds bloody ridiculous when you've just won 4-1 doesn't it!? No, it was just "we won 4-1", and 4-1 was a good win.

Perhaps some "grown-ups" were thinking that way back then and I didn't realise it, I don't know. Just takes me back to my earlier point about over-complicating things.

Sure, this game might not have been as comfortable as the score-line suggests, but at the end of the day that doesn't really matter. Three points do matter, and you get three points whether you win comfortably or uncomfortably. However, it seems the hot topic over the next day or two is discussing whether Iwobi played well or not. Some are saying he had a great game, even suggesting he was man of the match, compounded by the fact that he played a part in two goals.

Others are saying he was shit, because he's shit, and setting up two goals doesn't mean he's not shit.

I'm not really here to give player ratings, but in the spirit of the other theme of the week – trying not to overcomplicate things – what I will say is this; he can't possibly have been both.

Anyway, the "is Iwobi shit?" debate continued for the next couple of days, with the "can Aaron Ramsey be considered a legend?" debate brewing nicely in the background, with talk of him agreeing to sign for Juventus in the summer.

I can't quite fathom the level of vitriol that Iwobi gets from some quarters, to be honest, in the same way I never got it with Ramsey come to think of it. He's a youngster that came through the ranks, and he loves the club. If you don't rate him then that's your prerogative, but go easy on the lad eh? Next up…the magic of the FA Cup!

Saturday January 5th 2019
Blackpool 0 Arsenal 3

The FA Cup has been an extremely enjoyable competition for us in recent years. This time last year, however, was one of the worst displays I've seen by Arsenal in recent years, by the players on the pitch, and the manager that picked them.

That's in the past now, though. Forward we go.

There was good news early on for whoever had "1-2 minutes" in the "How Long Before They Mention the Liverpool Game?" sweepstake, as it was on around one minute fifty seconds, I think.

There was also a rather disturbing image on our screens, as it looked as if someone had dug up Peter Stringfellow and put a hat and shades on him. To my relief though, it turned out to be the Blackpool owner, the man that is responsible for what looks like half of the stadium being empty, as Blackpool fans stay away in protest of his ownership.

Those empty seats are a very sad sight. The FA Cup is supposed to be about games like this for clubs like Blackpool, and you can bet that if it were not for these protests, the ground would have been full to capacity.

As it was, we did a professional job, and never really looked in any danger, despite Blackpool having a few moments, and Mcmanamanamanamanaman doing his best to commentate the ball into the net for them.

Carl Jenkinson started his first FA Cup game for Arsenal for five years (I think), after Koscielny was injured in the warm up. One can only imagine the look on his little face when he got the word in his ear. Like a kid who was just told by his parents they were off to Disneyland in the morning, when he was expecting two-weeks in Great Yarmouth.

It was great to see some of the youngsters get a run out, Young Joe Willock – who scored twice - in particular. Job done, and in the hat for the next round it is then!

Week Twenty-Two, January 6th – 12th 2019
Crappy New Year

Monday morning, January 7th 2019. This is when the New Year really kicks in for most people. That "New Year, New Me" stuff that you posted on Facebook just under a week ago is already hanging by the most delicate of threads.

If you are one of the lucky ones, you might manage to drag a couple more days out of it, but the fact is that by around Wednesday afternoon it will seem like a distant memory as the world brutally crushes your spirit once more.

By Monday lunchtime you will have heard the words "Happy New Year" so many times that they have lost any meaning.

All you have to keep you going now is "Dry January", which you have decided to try yet again this year. You will do your best to fool people that you are doing it for the benefit of your health, when the reality is that you are doing it because the Christmas festivities have left you without a pot to piss in (this is why I am embarking on my own "Dry Until my January Payday.")

You now have to wait what seems like six months before your next payday, and you can't even drink your woes away. Happy New Year indeed. Still, it was nice while it lasted wasn't it?

With no midweek Arsenal action, we are forced to find something else to keep us entertained. But, guess what... it's that time of year again, folks... the Transfer Window.

For those of you that haven't experienced it; Twitter during the transfer window is something else. Thankfully, it isn't as bad as it was a few years ago, which I can only partially attribute to some of the weirdos who used to come out at this time of year either being arrested or discovering the opposite sex. Other than that, I think the more sensible among us take these people with a pinch of salt now. I am of course talking about our old friend the "ITK."

In case you didn't know already; ITK stands for "In the Know". What a bunch of C's. You can usually separate the ITKs into two categories.

There are the spotty little virgins that live with their parents, and somehow manage to fit spouting nonsense on Twitter in between unhealthily long spells on the PlayStation and masturbating into a sock. These can be spotted a mile off, but still attract the attention of seemingly sensible adults who don't realise that they have a scoring system in place for every time someone replies to their Tweets, be it deriding them or believing them.

One angry quote tweet = a round of Fortnite, one in the sock, and a Freddo bar. It really should go without saying, but these oddballs are best ignored. If you engage, you come out of it looking worse than they do.

"Good day at work, love?"

"Not bad. Spent most of my lunchbreak arguing with someone called The Transferinator on Twitter…" The second category are even more worrying in my opinion, at least the aforementioned spotty virgins don't actually believe their own nonsense.

These grown adults pretend to know what's going on behind the scenes at a football club that, at times, don't even seem to know what they're doing in the transfer market themselves. They will often tweet such phrases as "I'm hearing…" or "From what I've been told…" and such bollocks as that. For the life of me, I will never understand why people do this; it must be an illness of some kind. Go outside and make some real friends, weirdo.

The transfer window has given rise to some interesting theories over the years, but my favourite has to be the "smokescreen." A brief explanation of the smokescreen goes something like this:

One club, let's call them Club S, let it be leaked that they want to buy a player, who we will call player H, from another club, who for the sake of this example we will call club I. This is to alert yet another club, say, Club T, to take their attention away from the actual target, who turns out to be Player E. Put all those factors together and what do you get? SHITE. Exactly.

There are already dozens of "targets" floating about, most of them literally made up by people with nothing better to do. Later in the week, however, the manager decided to put us out of our misery early on, thus ruining January for Agent Wanksock et al, by announcing that Arsenal are unable to sign any players in January, only loan players in.

This, coupled with the fact that it seems Aaron Ramsey has indeed agreed to join Juventus in the summer, made for rather depressing news.

I'm hoping that Emery has been looking at Twitter reading all the nonsense that people have been putting out there and decided to go on a massive wind up (maybe it's a smokescreen!) and is sitting there laughing at us all, but I'm clutching at straws there.

One thing is for sure though; we are more than a little bit in the poo right now. I can't really bring myself to go into who may or may not be to blame for our current predicament. There are so many factors, I could be here all week.

Saturday January 12th, 2019
West Ham 1 Arsenal 0

Most of us have given Emery a free pass for this season, but it's safe to say that the honeymoon period is now well and truly over. We are now at the stage where we are farting in front of each other. If things get any worse, we'll be at the brushing our teeth while the other has a dump stage, then it may be time to suggest we see other people, seeing as we found out the other day that bringing someone else in to spice up the relationship is out of the question.

Make no mistake - this was bad. Very bad. Other than a few moments early on where we played some decent football in the final third, there was a complete lack of creativity and, at times, we looked as though we didn't know what we were doing or what we were supposed to be doing.

I really don't want to be too hard on Emery, but he got the team selection and tactics completely wrong today, and I'm afraid this one is on him. No Özil in the squad, Ramsey and Torreira on the bench. Wrong.

At least we continued the time-honoured tradition of allowing young players to make a name for themselves though, as Declan Rice scored his first goal since he was six years old playing in the park with jumpers for goalposts and rush goalie, making amends for missing a good chance in the first half.

When they got the free-kick from which the goal eventually came, I was actually tempted to stick the tenner I had in my Bet365 account on him scoring. I've never bet against Arsenal in my life, so I decided not to do so now and put it on a horse instead. It lost. That pretty much sums it up.

As much as I am prepared to give the new boss time, I would be lying if I said I wasn't beginning to have my doubts. Yes, it is very early days yet, and yes he deserves time to get things the way he wants them, but I see no problem in questioning the direction he is going in, or indeed if there is one. This doesn't mean I'm "turning on him." I tell you one thing, as well, I won't be told what I can and can't question by anyone who actually wanted Arsenal to lose last season in order to get rid of the last manager.

Week 23, January 13th – 19th, 2019
Roll up roll up! The Arsenal circus is back in town!

Monday morning, and whilst having a scroll through Twitter, I've had to double check the date, because it's as if I've woken up in 2017, with Wenger and Gazidis getting plenty of stick.

That fleeting visit from the mythical Unigooner is now nothing but a distant memory. If he was hanging around in the background in hope for us, I can only imagine he's thought to himself "sod that for a laugh" and hotfooted it back to 2004 whence he came.

It's no wonder he's done a runner when for the most part we cocked a collective snoot at him anyway. He must have raised an eyebrow when five minutes after he turned up, we were even arguing over singing, "We've got our Arsenal back" for fucks sake.

I've said it before, and I'll say it again – I blame the internet, particularly social media. I get the feeling that a united fanbase is impossible while some carry on as if they don't even want one, because it doesn't suit the online personas that they've created for themselves. Social media has turned us into some sort of shit, Poundland WWE.

We were never going to stay happy for too long though; who needs a united fanbase when you can argue instead? I've come to accept that being an Arsenal supporter is always going to be like this now.

Welcome back, apathy, my old friend.

I am now back to where I was at the beginning of the season. No expectations, no pressure, I'm just going to sit back and enjoy the ride, however bumpy it may be. I mean, life's too short to get stressed over it, right?

So here we are, a fanbase divided once more.

In fact, not only divided, we are fragmented. At least during the Wenger Wars it was a more straightforward "are you Wenger In or Wenger Out then?" (Just give me the toilet roll, man!)

Having said that, however, I think it's possible - and sensible - to ignore the lunatic fringes (I include those calling for the managers head in that.)

If we do that, we can narrow it down to two main groups; those that insist Emery needs time, money (haha yeah, I know) and a few transfer windows before we can really judge him, and those that are questioning some of his decisions, tactics, direction and indeed whether he's the right man for the job.

As far as I'm concerned, both of those viewpoints are valid, and there's no need for them to be mutually exclusive either. This was always going to be a long ride, and there were always going to be bumpy patches, so how do we ride it out?

Forget about the football, forget about the manager, and forget about the club. In fact, forget about anything you can't control; how do we fix this, as fans? How do we make this whole situation more bearable?

Yeah, I know what you're thinking, and my first thought was drink and drugs too, but I can't really advocate that here. I think the best thing is to take whatever good you can from supporting a football club, and not let the bad stuff drag you down.

Look at social media, for example. It symbolises everything I can't stand about the modern world and exposes you to a level of dickhead you never knew existed.

At the same time, however, I personally have made some very good friends through it, many of whom I've been lucky enough to meet.

It's here, it's not going away, so you might as well embrace it. You can hate it and embrace it at the same time too, that way you're taking what you want from it, rather than letting it take anything from you.

The same goes for football. Take what you can from it, because it sure as hell doesn't care what it takes from you.

There is enough doom and gloom in the world without letting football become a part of it. Anyway, sermon over.

Elsewhere, Chelsea legend Petr Cech announced that he is to hang up his helmet at the end of the season. He announced it on Twitter, with a statement he had apparently written in the Notes app on his iPhone, which for some reason I found quite endearing. The club then put out what looked like a rather rushed statement that looked as if they had just seen it on Twitter themselves. One can only imagine the panic among the club's social media team.

"He's tweeted what?? Oh FFS..." (Yes, I imagine that social media people talk in abbreviations and emojis.) "Right, you; put off posting that interview with Hector about bouncing back against Chelsea for now... and you; get on Wikipedia and check how many clean sheets he's kept. What? LMAO... No don't be silly, include the Chelsea ones as well FFS..."

The "drama" continued throughout the week, with rumours that Sven Mislintat may be leaving the club. I'm not sure I've ever trusted him anyway; his name looks like it's an anagram.

Naturally, the reaction to this was way, way over the top to say the least, with theories flying about all over the place. I'm staying out of this one, firstly because I have no idea what's going on behind the scenes, and secondly because, once again, I'm getting bored with it all.

I have deliberately not mentioned the Ozil situation this week, because that's starting to bore me as well. Moreover, there's also the fact that if I were to mention it, then I would be here all week talking about something that, ultimately, none of us actually know about.

Chelsea at home next, then. The first in a run of difficult fixtures, which could have a big impact on how our season pans out. The hashtag given to this battle of the transitional periods is #ARSCHE, which is dangerously close to "Arse ache." Let's hope that isn't a sign of things to come.

Saturday January 19th, 2019
Arsenal 2 Chelsea 0

For as long as I can remember, The Arsenal have had this knack of pulling off a performance and a result when you don't see it coming.

An Arsenal side including Eboue and Senderos, with Flamini at left back, beating Real Madrid at the Bernabeu is one that immediately springs to mind, but there have been many more. Enough that I can't remember them all, put it that way.

I suppose you could include Anfield '89 in that too. It's easy now to look back and say you believed we could do it, but you can't tell me you thought that way when you walked out of Highbury after we drew 2-2 with Wimbledon before that fateful night. I certainly didn't.

I've seen us do this so many times over the years, with completely different personnel, that I can only assume it's some kind of sorcery that pulls you back in just as you're beginning to have your doubts. This was one of those occasions.

I was starting to have some major doubts too, as I alluded to last week, and I was critical of Emery, both during and after the game. This week though, he got it spot on. This was being billed as a "must-win" game for us, and it was hard to disagree with that.

Two first half goals were enough to seal it, even if Chelsea did have a lot of the ball in the second half, they lacked the firepower up top for it to make a difference.

Lacazette's goal was superb, and how great was it to see Koscielny get the second (off of his shoulder) after the injury nightmare he's had?

You could see how much that goal, and this result, meant to him too. I can't for the life of me understand some of the stick Kos gets from some Arsenal fans. He's been a great servant to the club, even playing through the pain barrier with bits of his body held together with gaffer tape at times. Anyway, as far as I'm concerned it was great to see him score and celebrate in the way he did, after all those years he had to shoulder the defensive burden.

Once again, though, a serious injury overshadowed our victory, this time to Hector Bellerin. He went down in the second half with what looked like a nasty knee injury. If it's as bad as it looked, then that will be three players side-lined for the season, including half of what might be our best back four. I have a bad feeling that this one might really hurt us as well. Our main concern always has to be the welfare of the player, however, so get well soon, Hector! So, the Arsenal rollercoaster rolls on.

Week Twenty-Four, January 20th – 26th, 2019
Blue Monday, Bad Friday

Today is Blue Monday, apparently "the most depressing day of the year." In 2005, a psychologist named Dr Cliff Arnall came up with a scientific formula to explain this completely made up phenomenon, which is frankly an insult to anyone that has genuinely suffered from depression. I prefer the New Order version personally anyway.

The formula is as follows: "[W+(D-d)]xTQ/MxNA – where W is weather, D is debt, d monthly salary, T time since Christmas, Q time since failure of attempt to give something up, M low motivational level and NA the need to take action."

I could have saved him the effort and done that myself. It's the 98th of January. It's been so long since my last payday that I've started to feel like I don't actually get paid to work. It's freezing bloody cold and I am dying for a beer. I don't need a weatherman to tell me it's peeing down, Mr Psychologist.

It really is amazing what difference a win can make, and while we're not exactly skipping around arm-in-arm whistling "zip a dee doo dah", the mood among the fans has lifted somewhat. Of course, not everybody is happy with that; some people seem weirdly offended by others being happy, but there you go.

The club officially announced that Sven the Anagram is to leave the club with possibly the most underwhelming article ever published on the internet.

We are a bit calmer after the win over Chelsea though, and I think this is a great example of the effect the result of a match has on how you view things. A few bad results and Sven leaving was major news, then we beat Chelsea and most of us are all a bit "meh…" about it.

There was genuine bad news when the extent of Hector's knee injury was confirmed, and he now faces a 6-9 month lay-off. I'm gutted for him, as is everyone else it seems. Apart from the credit card companies. You can order a whole load of nutty clobber online over 6-9 months. Meanwhile, Unai decided the squad needed a bit of a bonding session and took them all out paintballing. You can imagine how that went.

The squad meet up outside the venue, to find Sokratis already kitted up in all the gear – fatigues, body armour, goggles, the lot.

"You been in there already, Papa?"

"No. I brought this from home."

There follows an awkward silence and a lot of nervous looks, before Emery claps his hands.

"Okay, let me ESPLAIN what we are doing today."

He motions to Steve Bould, who reaches into one of two large holdalls by his feet. He pulls out a laptop and hands it to the boss, who in turn reaches into his pocket and pulls out a USB stick. He proceeds to open up a spreadsheet from a folder entitled "Team Building 1 – Paintball."

After the squad are separated into teams, the gaffer gives a little speech... "The purpose of today is for us to all work together as a team, to work for each other. Some of you, will be more suited to this than others..." he pauses and looks up at the squad, each and every one of whom immediately stare at the floor and shuffle awkwardly, in the way that people do when a couple is having a domestic in front of them.

"But I expect ALL OF YOU..." another pause, another look up, more awkward shuffling and downward glances...

"I expect all of you to put the same amount of effort in..."

As for the paintballing itself... There's always one that runs around like an absolute lunatic, getting shot left, right and centre; you would have to think that would be Guendouzi.

Sokratis and Kolasinac would have to be on different teams, to prevent an absolute bloodbath that would spell an end to our season.

Those two would simply march slowly through a barrage of paintballs, not flinching when hit and with nobody daring to tell them that they have to go back to the respawn area, until they meet in the middle and fight to the death. Lichtsteiner is the sly one that spends most of the time hiding, before creeping up behind you seconds before the round is up and shooting you up the arse.

Then there's good old Gooner Jenko - with his uniform tucked into his Arsenal socks – who sees this as the perfect opportunity to get some game time during Bellerin's injury lay-off. He sets out to go straight after Maitland-Niles, but this turns out to be unnecessary as he's not sure which position he's supposed to be taking up and wanders off into the forest. Unfortunately for Jenks, he has less joy with Lichtsteiner, and spends the rest of the day with a paintball lodged up his bum.

As for Özil and Emery, they're on the same team, all forced smiles and banter, even going to the trouble of a selfie or two, but you can cut the tension with a knife. You can bet that Unai didn't turn his back on him once.

(I could honestly do this all day, but there's a big game coming up on Friday, so I'll leave it there...)

Friday - I've been looking forward to this evening all week. Payday yesterday, and after eating well and not having a beer since New Year's Day, I've had plans in place for a beer, pizza and The Arsenal night since they announced the date of the game.

As I sit here and write this at 7pm, waiting for the pizza to turn up, the nerves have started to kick in a bit. You know how after the Chelsea game, I mentioned how often Arsenal have pulled a result off when you are least expecting it? Well, there are probably as many occasions they have dropped their shorts and crapped on an otherwise great day / night, particularly one you have been looking forward to.

FA Cup ties against United always evoke memories, both good and bad.

The best of them being Brian McClair launching that penalty into the packed North Bank. The worst of course is that semi-final replay in '99. That still hurts for a lot of us. Oh, Dennis. Why???

Someone asked me this afternoon how I think tonight's game will go. My answer, as seems to have been the case for as long as I can remember now was; "Not a fucking clue. Depends what Arsenal turns up..." How many of you have said that in recent years?

Friday January 25th, 2019
Arsenal 1 Manchester United 3

Honestly, they're like clockwork, aren't they? Pizza was lovely, and the beer tasted even better after a few weeks without one, but that's about as good as the evening got.

It just had to be Alexis that got the first goal as well didn't it? Followed by Jesse bloody Lingard doubling their lead and proceeding to moonwalk around like a massive twat. Things couldn't have got any worse if the cat jumped up and pooped on my pepperoni.

Fate then decided that we don't have enough defenders out at the moment, and Sokratis injured his ankle and joined the rest of them. This meant shifting Xhaka to centre-half. Marvellous. We still managed to pull one back through Aubameyang, after superb work from Ramsey.

Half time was great fun, as some funny fucker at the BBC thought it would be a good idea to relive THAT night in '99 again. Okay, this year may be the 20th anniversary of that game, but it's also the 40th anniversary of the time we beat them 3-2 in the final, but nobody was in a bloody rush to interview Brian Talbot and Alan Sunderland, were they?

I thought we looked more like scoring once Özil came on, but inevitably we were caught on the break, Cech parried a shot straight to Martial, and that was that.

Our reaction to the goal that was the final nail in our FA Cup coffin was... interesting. It seemed to give everyone the opportunity to blame the player they don't like, and I saw Xhaka, Özil, Cech and Iwobi slaughtered in the outrage that followed.

Out of those, only Cech I can understand, but the others are a common target and their mere presence on the pitch is enough for them to feel the ire of the fans these days.

Lacazette in fact gave the ball away in the build-up to the goal, but I'm not sure I saw him mentioned at all!

I really can't be bothered to play the blame game tonight, though.

Their fans are singing Robin Van Persie's name and that poxy Vieira song, Lingard is prancing about on our pitch, and we are out of the FA Cup. Manchester United are laughing at us in our own backyard just as Tottenham were last month and, tonight, I hate everyone. Blue Monday? Happy bloody Friday.

Week Twenty-Five, Jan 27th – Feb 2nd, 2019
Top Four's Our Everything

It didn't take me too long to calm down after Friday's result. Once I had slept on it, I was able to look at it with a bit more perspective. We all react in the heat of the moment over football and we all hate losing. I still hate losing to Man United as much as I did back in the Wenger v Fergie days, when it was United and us battling it out for honours. That loss in '99 is still one of the most painful, so I think them knocking us out of the cup rubs salt in an old wound that still hasn't fully healed.

Looking at the result a day or two later, though, and the fact that we lost two defenders from an already decimated defence, well, we are not the only team that would struggle after that. Of course, there is the fact that we still have big problems defensively even when at full strength, but defenders dropping like flies is hardly going to help us improve in that respect. Anyway, the FA Cup is gone for another season now, and there's nothing we can do about it.

We don't have to wait too long until the next game. It's not as if beating Cardiff at home will make Friday's result any easier to take, but it's all we have at the moment. I've decided to put all of this season's eggs in Unai's Europa League basket. Perhaps that has been his plan all along. He does have a good record in the competition after all, and let's face it, we haven't really seen any other semblance of a plan in the last few weeks. Still, forward we go... Cardiff at home it is then...

Tuesday January 29th, 2019
Arsenal 2 Cardiff City 1

There are occasions when the result of a football match pales into insignificance. This is one of them. The disappearance of the plane carrying Cardiff's new signing - Argentine striker Emiliano Sala – along with the pilot David Ibbotson, certainly puts the game into perspective.

Second half goals from Lacabameyang sealed the win for us, with 'Bameyang putting us ahead from the spot, before Laca doubled our lead with a superb strike on 83 minutes. Cardiff pulled one back in the closing minutes of the game.

Not a vintage performance by any stretch, but once again; you can't ask for any more than three points. (Well, technically you can ask for more – you just can't get any more.)

It was nice to see Jenko managing to get that paintball dislodged from his rectum in time to get some Premier League minutes under his belt again after so long too.

With Bellerin out for a long spell, Lichtsteiner being 800 years old, and AMN apparently still wandering round in the woods in full paintball attire, there's a chance we might need to call on him in the coming months. One thing you can be sure of is that he will give 100% every time he wears the red and white. I don't think you can ask for more than that. (Well, technically you can ask for more, but nobody can give more than 100%, because by definition that is the most anyone can give.)

Later in the week, Chelsea were hilariously thumped 4-0 by Bournemouth, meaning we moved into the top four on goal differ-ence. If this had been a certain club up the road, the media would no doubt be lauding Pochettino for being the first Argentine man-ager ever to reach a Champions League spot without kicking a ball.

I remain convinced that the sports media have all been offered exclusive membership to the new cheese lounge once that lot finally manage to move into their new gaff.

How long our spell in the top four will last is anyone's guess, seeing as we face Manchester City at the Etihad on Sunday. This upcoming fixture means that the next few days are awash with the usual side-splitting tweets joking about how many goals City will beat us by. Oh, the #banter.

Week Twenty-Six, February 3rd – 9th, 2019
Whiney Unhappy People

We begin week twenty-six in the same way we began this story - this new era; playing Manchester City. I must say, it seems a million miles away from those halcyon days of August 2018. Our expecta-tions are still low, but that air of resignation has replaced one of optimism. Whereas back then we were excited by the beginning of this new era and where it might take us, today we are worried about how much of a thrashing we are going to get.

As fans, we are now completely back to where we were at the end of last season; at each other's throats. We have something new to argue about on what seems like a daily basis, and you know what? That's exactly how so many Arsenal fans seem to want it to be.

As I alluded to last week, we have people that don't seem to want to be happy, and people that don't seem to want other people being happy. It is genuinely astonishing when you look at how football and social media have led grown adults to behave.

I apologise if that sounds a bit holier than thou - it's not intended that way - and in all honesty, I've been guilty of it myself. Most of us have.

I could go on about this a lot more, but what we have is basically just a continuation of the AKB / WOB nonsense. The uneasy truce that accompanied that unbeaten run earlier in the season is well and truly broken (let's face it, it was all bollocks anyway), and once again we are split into two sides slinging poop at each other, while the unlucky few trying to mind their own business in no-man's land are showered with it.

I would say that playing City is a good opportunity to measure what progress we have, or haven't, made since the beginning of the season, but everyone seems to have their own spin on progress at the moment so it's hardly worth the effort.

Sunday February 3rd, 2019
Manchester City 3 Arsenal 1

My usual blind optimism was crushed in under a minute, which is all it took for Aguero and his ridiculous hair to give City the lead.

Funnily enough, we equalised from a corner, when Koscielny played Tony Adams to Monreal's Steve Bould. We even played some decent enough stuff up until a superb example of Arsenal defending, mainly from Lichsteiner, saw Aguero net his second and put us behind again just before half-time. That was that, really.

Christ knows what we got up to at half time, as we came out looking more knackered than we were when we went in.

Aguero brought up his hattrick by handballing into the Arsenal net, but in truth the manner of the goal didn't make much difference, as City looked as if they could step up a gear at their leisure.

Gary Neville called it "contentious", but his tone was one of "look, lads, it was handball, but just let them have that one and they might leave off you a bit, yeah?"

There was one thing that I found so tragically amusing in the second half though, and that was when Denis Suarez came on as a sub for his Arsenal debut. Why was this amusing? Well, the poor kid looked absolutely fucking petrified. Honestly, he trotted onto the pitch with the demeanour of a kid that had just got off the bus at the wrong stop.

Neville actually managed to sum up precisely where New Arsenal are at the moment with one rhetorical question in the second half, when he asked "What do you do now if you're City? Do you just see out the game, or do you go for 4,5 or 6 and really send a message to Liverpool?" (Words to that effect anyway.)

As painful as that sounds, it's where we are now. We need to accept it, if we haven't already. This was always going to be a long ride, and this is just a gigantic bump in the road along the way.

Also, this long ride that we are on; nobody said it wouldn't be completed without a change of driver along the way.

It's probably best we just don't distract the dude holding the steering wheel at the moment, though.

Personally, I don't see a problem with discussing, among ourselves, the route he's taking; after all, we just want to get where we are going. After years of driving around in circles, it's only natural to be impatient.

As I've said before, I'm generally a positive person. Well, at least, I try to be. I honestly think that trying to find the positives in a situation - or if that's not possible, then at least putting the negatives into some kind of perspective - helps you to live a better quality of life. Negativity, arguing, anger; they're all just such a drain on your spirit. Exhausting, and often utterly pointless.

Trust me, I've been there. I've been in a place where all you can focus on is the negative. It's unhealthy.

Positivity breeds belief, and in turn gives you a better outlook on life and sometimes, sometimes, that leads to a change in luck.

I'm not saying you're some kind of weirdo mental case if you get wound up by football, by the way.

It's probably quite the opposite, in fact, as long as you can separate football from real life.

I was feeling pretty negative about The Arsenal yesterday.

I've been having my doubts about the new manager.

Today, I'm over it. Just taking a look at some of the ridiculous (yet, sadly, predictable) extremes there are out there has helped me.

So, thank you. You lovely mad bastards.

The rest of the week was taken up by the petty squabbling and one-upmanship we've had to endure for God knows how long. It's pretty much the kind of crap that caused me to give up writing about it in the first place, so I have made the decision to do just that for a few days.

Saturday February 9th, 2019
Huddersfield Town 1 Arsenal 2

An away win. Something that was hard to come by last season. Something to smile about? Nah, this is Arsenal, so it's just something else for us to argue about.

This time last year, we had Arsenal fans that wanted the team to lose, so they could get themselves a shiny new manager.

Now, some of the same people are having a go at anyone that "moans after we win a game", and some people are looking for reasons to moan after we've won a game. The whole Arsenal universe has flipped on its head and somehow managed to be no different at the same time.

I really can't be bothered with it all. It hurts my head a bit when I think about it, to be honest! Iwobi and Lacazette were our goalscorers. I'll come back to this next week.

Week Twenty-Seven, February 10th – 16th, 2019
**If You (pretend you're going to) Build it,
They Will Come (and moan about it)**

Right, I'm not having any of it this week.

Emery vs Özil.

Have we progressed from last season?

Is Iwobi shit?

Who's the best Arsenal fan in the universe?

All of these, and whatever else this week's outrage is; you can shove the lot of them right up your arse for now. Put it this way – when the time comes that the club photographer has to put out tweets asking "fans" to stop sending online abuse to young players, it's most certainly time to move on. It's all got way too serious lately, so it's time to have a bit of fun.

If you've followed me on Twitter, you may know that I'm partial to a fake quote here, a fake article there, that kind of thing. I do this for no other reason than it being a bit of a laugh, if I'm honest. I suppose it could be used as a kind of social experiment as well, though. (Or a social media experiment, at least.)

Often, if I tweet one of these things out and someone falls for it, I will get asked "how do you STILL catch people with these????"

My answer is usually that it's all in the timing, and it really is. I'm not out to make anyone look stupid (although if that cap fits, obviously), but to make a point; people will believe anything if it gives them the chance to vent their internet rage. This is Arsenal. They were never going to make the "having a bit of fun" thing easy for me, were they?

The official announcement of Aaron Ramsey's departure for Juventus came through early in the week, met with the now unsurprising contrast in opinions from the fans. These ranged from people that genuinely seemed as if they need to be on suicide watch, to IF THEY DON'T WANNA PLAY FOR THE ARSENAL THEY CAN FAAAAAK ORRRRFFFF!!!! Amazingly, though, there is also this strange phenomenon where almost ALL Arsenal fans agreed on something; Aaron Ramsey leaving the club on a free transfer is ridiculous. Not rocket science, I know, but for a fanbase that have in the past been known to argue over at what age someone becomes 29, you have to take all you can get.

Of course, there was the usual "blame game" that we get with everything these days, although I think that's quite understandable in this particular situation.

It's been reported that Ramsey will be getting £400k a week. It's also been reported that he'll be getting £250k. Either way, he won't be going short of a few bob. It's interesting how the mere mention of £400k has made some people react. It's actually clickbait at its finest - because it may actually be true! (I don't think it is though, for what it's worth.)

Most people are only going to see that number. There is something about a heading, sub-heading or opening paragraph of a story containing a large amount of money that will cause our brains to temporarily cease functioning properly. I reckon you could literally begin an article like this;

"Aaron Ramsey doorbell Juventus willy-warmer £400K PER WEEK two all-beef patties special sauce lettuce cheese pickled onions on a sesame seed bun." ...and people would still go, "FOUR HUNDRED GRAND A WEEK?? NO WAY IS HE WORTH THAT!!!!!!!!!"

"Is that true though? I heard it's £250k?"

"NO IT MUST BE £400K COS THAT'S A BIGGER NUMBER!!!!"

Then all of a sudden, everyone becomes a fucking tax expert....

The "is Aaron Ramsey an Arsenal legend?" debate, which had been quietly bubbling below the surface for a number of months, of course came to the boil from this. Always great fun, that is.

With this in mind, and despite my disappointment at the confirmation of Ramsey's departure, the timing was right. I knocked up a mock article from the Arsenal website (honestly, it didn't even come close to looking genuine!) Here it is:

"The club are delighted to announce that a new statue is to be commisssioned, to be placed outside the Emirates Stadium. The statue will be created by renowned sculptor Anna Linjection, and we want you, the fans, to be involved. A shortlist has been drawn up by an independent panel, and fans will get to vote for the winner from the three iconic images as shown above. Departing Welsh legend Aaron Ramsey's celebration after scoring the FA Cup Final winner that ended the club's infamous "trophy drought" is sure to be a popular choice, and who can forget Olivier Giroud's sensational scorpion kick goal against Crystal Palace? The final option is Per Mertesacker and Theo Walcott's now legendary 'bump' celebration, which will mean that two club legends will join together for one statue. More details on how fans will be able to vote will be available soon."

I tweeted this (including the word "commissioned" unintentionally spelled with three "s's" which, amazingly, still nobody has noticed), with a comment on how good it was that the club were getting fans involved, and not long later... BINGO! People were believing it.

People were believing the next Emirates statue was to come from these three choices. One of which was Per Mertesacker and Theo Walcott in mid-air. By a sculptor named Anna Linjection. The reactions ranged from disbelief to complete outrage. A few hours later, I searched on Twitter for "arsenal statue", and people were discussing the "fact" that Arsenal were canvassing fans for their opinion, with many giving their own. Great fun.

So, was my statue "article" Clickbait? I'll leave that to you to decide, seeing as you've bought my book!

In my defence, though, I was doing stuff like that before I'd even thought about writing this book. Even before Fake News was an actual thing.

The best examples are when these things cross over into real life.

There was a time when a certain someone - who shall remain nameless - attributed a quote to a certain ex-footballer, that suggested that said footballer admitted to being drunk when signing for a certain London club.

Most of this person's followers were aware that this player hadn't actually said that, but within minutes this "quote" had been retweeted hundreds of times. So, this person bottled it big time and deleted the tweet, just in case.

A week or so later, the person responsible for the tweet received a direct message from a follower, who had been out to dinner with his father. At some point during the conversation that evening, Dad asked "did you hear about REDACTED? Apparently, he was drunk when he signed for REDACTED."

Marvellous.

Ah, Fake News. If the internet gave birth to Clickbait, then Fake News is Clickbait's bastard offspring.

These two are often mistaken for each other, such is the family resemblance.

So, what's the difference? To be honest, I'm not even sure there is much of one. They often work in cahoots.

For example, I'm sure if you dug deep enough into most of the fake news that is spread around on Facebook, you would find that it originated from a page that links to a website full of ads and affiliate links. I'm taking an educated guess here; I've not actually looked into it. I'm not insane.

My own personal motivation for throwing out the odd fake article here and the odd fake quote there is that this kind of thing fascinates me. People's reactions fascinate me (well, they do to a degree anyway.)

Back in the day, Fake News was known simply as "bollocks."

People have always believed bollocks, don't get me wrong. Nowadays, however, such is our need for outrage and drama, people will believe almost anything – it's outrage first, think later. Whilst there are people out there that will believe anything, there will be people out there that are willing to exploit it, be it for financial gain, or just to have a bloody good laugh.

At the end of the day; if people didn't react to Fake News and Clickbait, then you wouldn't be reading this, as I wouldn't have written it!

Going back to the "legend" thing, I do find it amusing just how angry some people get about it. The way I see it, there are two ways of settling this debate. The first one is to elect an Arsenal Legends Committee - made up of a typical cross-section of Arsenal fans from around the globe - to set the criteria that needs to be fulfilled in order to confirm who is and who isn't an Arsenal legend. Here are just a few of the committee members we could have.

The Arsenal Legends Committee

Before I go on, (and seeing as you have to explain everything these days!) this is just a bit of fun. It's not meant to be offensive to anyone. I think a lot of us tick a few boxes in more than one of these anyway... I know I do!

Old School Arsenal

Staunch AMF. Hates everything about the modern game. Calls the Emirates "the soulless bowl" and wishes we had never left Highbury. Loves a pair of Adidas trainers and keeps them all in the boxes.

Likely legend Criteria: Loves the club. Wasn't afraid to "put themselves about." Scored a few against Spurs. "One of us". Played at least one game pissed.

Look at Me!

Lives by a carefully compiled set of other people's opinions, refreshed daily. Like a Twitter version of "Indecisive Dave" from The Fast Show. Spends every morning meticulously scouring Twitter for today's popular "hot takes", then prepares his or her own tweets accordingly, in a desperate attempt to "fit in."

Being popular among people on the internet, whom they are unlikely to meet, is so important to them that they have forgotten how to converse with actual people in real-life.

Likely legend criteria: Will have to check what everyone else thinks.

The Statto

Lives a life totally dominated by stats. If it can't be calculated on a spreadsheet, it never happened. Could dig out a stat to prove anything to you. Firm believer that "xG" is more important than what actual people can see with their actual eyes, and probably believes that in years to come, football matches will not be decided on the pitch, but by a complex formula programmed into Microsoft Excel.

Likely legend Criteria: Just whack a few numbers in and see who comes out on top.

The Smart-Arse Blogger

An expert on every single formation known to man, including a few they have made up themselves. Analyses every minute of every game. Will often throw in some outrageous curveball, insisting we should sign a player who's actually quite shit, but will try to convince you, in 2,500 or so words, how he would fit into a certain "system." Will never come straight out with this, but is convinced that they themselves will be a football manager one day.

Likely legend Criteria: An "unsung hero", probably a right back. Someone from the 70s even your dad thinks was shit.

Imagine getting that lot together!

The second option is for everyone to accept that we live in a day and age that this is an entirely subjective, eye of the beholder type situation.

I'm going to stick my neck out here and suggest we plump for the latter, for the sake of everyone's sanity.

After all, one man's Ray Parlour is another man's Eboue.

Anyway, time for some football!

Thursday February 14th, 2019
BATE Borisov 1 Arsenal 0

BATE Borisov. Before tonight, most notable for the fact that you can't type their name without shouting.

BATE is an acronym of Borisov Automobile and Tractor Electronics. So, their full name is Borisov Automobile and Tractor Electronics Borisov. Not only do they have no netiquette, but they also repeat themselves. They make tractors, they shout, and they repeat themselves. This team beat us 1-0. We lost 1-0 to a team that make tractors. Or something.

Ozil wasn't in the squad, once more igniting the Ozil vs Emery nonsense. The only thing I have to say about that at the moment is this; would that team tonight have been better or worse with Mesut Ozil on the pitch?

I know what I think. Still, it's all about opinions, I guess.

As much as Arsenal should not be losing to a team like Borisov Automobile and Tractor Electronics Borisov – and make no mistake, this was just not good enough tonight – there is every chance we will beat them well enough in the second leg at home to go through and, ultimately, render this result academic. Here's hoping we pull our finger out next week, because this season will have gone so far south we'll end up somewhere in Cornwall.

Week Twenty-Eight, February 17th – 23rd, 2019
Emery vs Ozzzzzzzzzil……

Some great news to start the week off. On Monday evening, I had a meeting with Dave from Legends Publishing. The outcome of this meeting means that you are actually reading this, rather than it forever residing in the "Shattered_Dreams" folder in my Dropbox. A folder containing numerous failed job applications, a draft petition for a button that confirms I accept ALL the cookies on ALL the websites, and the plans for what was to be the invention that changed the world – The Self Opening Corned Beef Tin.

A title for this epic tome has also been finalised, after I had chopped and changed it a number of times.

I was originally going to call it "Forward – The Season Diary of an Arsenal Fan, 2018/19", but with where we are as a club and as fans, and the constant need for people to question EVERYTHING, I eventually thought "fuck that." Come to think of it, "Fuck That - The Season Diary of an Arsenal Fan, 2018/19" seems quite apt at this moment in time.

Once again, I am ignoring the Emery vs Ozil nonsense for the simple reason that, inevitably, it's boring me shitless. There isn't much point banging on about it anyway, as everyone has already made up their minds what "side" they're on. Unsurprisingly, the "sides" haven't altered a great deal from this time last year, it's just that the central figure in it all has changed.

Okay, this whole thing isn't a good situation overall for Arsenal Football Club to be in, and it's actually a bit embarrassing.

Mesut deciding now would be a good time to put out a Tweet quoting Dennis Bergkamp, in what was quite obviously a dig at the manager, has only made things worse. (Although speaking as someone that would probably Tweet something similar if I were in his boat I did have a little chuckle.)

I think the best way to look at it is; if Mesut Ozil plays, and Mesut Ozil plays well, it's good for Arsenal. Perhaps they need to sit down and talk things through with some outside help.

"Today on the Jeremy Kyle Show... Mesut says that his boss is deliberately freezing him out from doing his job. Mesut's boss, Unai, insists that Mesut is lazy, and needs to work as hard as his teammates to be given a chance... Mesut is on the Jeremy Kyle show, ladies and gentleman..."

Mesut ambles his way onto the stage, shoulders hunched. Half of the audience are booing and the other half giving are on their feet giving him a rousing ovation.

"So, Mesut, tell me what's going on..."

"Well, Jeremy, I....." his voice starts to break up, "sorry... this is hard for me."

"Ok, in your own time"

"I'm doing all that I can... I'm working hard and I'm...."

"YOU *BEEPING* LYING LITTLE *BEEP* YOU *BEEP* *BEEP* *BEEEEEEEEEEP* I *BEEEEEP* MY *BEEEEEEEEP* *BEEEEEEEEEEEEEP*"

"Oi! You'll get your chance in a minute, stay back there and keep your mouth shut... this is called The Jeremy Kyle Show, you know!"

Yeah, maybe not.

There you go; I've told you that I'm ignoring it, then proceeded to write 306 words on it. Fucks sake.

As I sit here on the day of the second leg of the Europa tie with the shouty tractor boys, I have managed to find a positive. That positive is the fact that I actually have a bit of a buzz going on about this game.

We still have a European trophy to play for, and the Europa League is now more than just a consolation for not qualifying for the Champions League, but a tiny speck of light at the end of the tunnel that has been the last couple of months. The fact that it kicks off at 5.55pm in London (how fucking ludicrous is that?) which means there might only be half a dozen people at the game hardly makes it a glamour tie, I know, but it's all we've got just now.

Thursday February 21st, 2019
Arsenal 3 BATE Borisov 0

An early goal is exactly what you need in a tie like this, and that's exactly what we got courtesy of an own goal on four minutes. Apparently, this was our fastest goal in European competition since Lukas Podolski's strike against Galatasaray in December 2014, and I believe it's the only time we have led a game 1-0 before the end credits of The Chase had finished.

The much-maligned Mustafi (which I'm told is actually his nickname among the squad) doubled our lead five minutes before the break, putting us in "we're winning but if they score we could be fucked" territory. Thankfully, Sokratis gave us some breathing space on the hour mark – after only being on the pitch for 226 seconds – and that turned out to be enough.

Job done and we can now file the first-leg loss under "Results That Ended up Being Meaningless", alongside that time we beat Barcelona 2-1 (ARSHAVIIIIIINNNN!) that is still, for some reason, lauded every year.

Oh, and Mesut Ozil started the game tonight, meaning he must have run an extra few yards in training, or whatever, this week.

Week Twenty-Nine Feb 24th – Mar 2nd, 2019
Seven Points, One Offside, a Missed Penalty and Saturday Night with Sam Wallace

A busy week coming up, culminating in the last North London Derby of the season, at... hang on... Wembley. Yeah, they're still playing home games at Wembley... while they put the finishing touches to whatever will replace what was to be the cheese room.

Seriously, lads, I know we took the piss, but to deny the people their Stinking Bishop after getting their hopes up for so long; there's no need for that. (In case you were wondering; Stinking Bishop is a "sicky, medium-soft cheese, originally made by monks and is mild and scoffable", apparently.)

What a bunch of Boerenkaas. (YES, I'VE BEEN GOOGLING CHEESE.)

It is nice to have a busy week ahead of the NLD. It means we can focus our attention firmly on the fixtures directly ahead of us before the dreaded butterflies begin around Thursday afternoon sometime. With that in mind, it's time to forget about cheese and focus on the first game this week.

Sunday February 24th, 2019
Arsenal 2 Southampton 0

Okay, I know I was going to forget about that lot, but watching The World's Greatest Ever Trophyless Manager completely lose his rag with The World's Biggest Dickhead of a Referee, after going down 2-1 at Burnley earlier in the day, was the perfect start to the week. That great start continued with a 2-0 home win in the sun, on an abnormally hot February afternoon.

A great first-half performance saw us 2-0 up after 17 minutes, with Lacazette and Mkhitaryan the goalscorers.

Another welcome clean sheet as well, with Leno making some good saves to keep Southampton out.

A good day all round, and everyone went home that little bit happier today.

A couple of tidy wins on the trot + laughing at Tottenham + feelings of early springtime = happy Arsenal fans.

The positive side of climate change.

Maybe it's been the weather that has been affecting our moods these last few months all along, a touch of SAD (Seasonal Arsenal Disorder?) going around.

I wonder if there's any way we can build some kind of weather simulator in the Emirates? Mind you, it's not only match-goers that are responsible for the mood amongst the fanbase, so perhaps someone could develop and app of some kind as well?

A little later on, we also got the chance to laugh at Chelsea, as their keeper... erm... Kepa, refused to leave the pitch when Sarri attempted to substitute him just before the game went to penalties. Which they then proceeded to lose.

I actually had a fleeting moment of sympathy for Sarri, until I remembered that he is manager of Chelsea Football Club, and then I laughed a bit more.

Then I realised that I was laughing at one billionaire's plaything being beaten by another billionaire's plaything, which reminded me just how much I hate modern football, and the fact that we may never again see such a thing as a level playing field. Then I realised that I would rather Manchester City - the club that are the epitome of this situation - win the league, purely because I don't want Liverpool to win it, which made me want to do a little bit of sick in my mouth. Then my thoughts turned once more to Pochettino losing his shit with Mike Dean earlier in the day, and I laughed a bit more.

A pleasant Monday morning, then. I find myself in a good mood, partly due to the weekend's events football-wise, but also because this is my last week in my current job. A job I have been trying to escape from for as long as I can remember. So long, in fact, that I'm not even thinking about the aforementioned upcoming brown-trouser derby, as I am going to do my best to enjoy the week, and by enjoy I obviously mean do as little work as possible, and by as little work as possible, I obviously mean "fuck all."

Apparently, this is also the hottest Monday in February since records began. If this Monday were Tottenham Hotspur, Sky Sports would be tweeting about it, and Matt Law would be writing an article about it that somehow found an angle to wind up Arsenal fans.

Ironically, there is something of a climate change among the Arsenal fanbase, as we begin the week collectively more chilled than we have been in a while.

Obviously, getting a couple of wins under our belt has helped, but the early part of the week also sees us united in having a good laugh at others.

The astonishing scenes at Wembley on Sunday are at the fore-front of this, because laughing at Chelsea is fun. The thought of one day laughing at Chelsea again was all that kept me going during Mourinho's first spell at the club, when he was beating Arsenal and winning titles, rather than shouting at female staff and trying to get himself the sack.

In all seriousness though, player power such as this is potentially dangerous. Imagine if this had happened a year or two ago when Arsene was still at Arsenal, and he would stand up to make his standard 70th minute substitution, only to find that every Arsenal player on the pitch had begun an impromptu game of hide and seek?

Kepa the 'keeper was fined and forced to apologise. I don't see why that should be the case... he's given us all a bloody good laugh after all. His apology on Twitter made us all laugh a bit more, it was along the lines of "Well, Doctor, I was hoovering naked and I just sort of slipped onto the hose attachment, thus my penis was somehow sucked into it..."

On top of that, we have The Trophyless One's hilarious antics on Saturday to entertain ourselves with. It's quite clear that Mike Dean said something when confronted by "Poch" after the final whistle, whatever it was, it obviously hit a raw nerve, judging by the reactions of Poch and Jesus Perez. There are rumours going around what that was exactly, with the most popular of these being that he said something about bottling the title again.

I think we can be a bit more creative than that though, don't you?

"Not being funny, lads, but I'm Mike Dean. You are actually making yourselves look bigger twats than me, Mike Dean."

"Wait... your name's Jesus? Wow, you used to keep way better company..."

We may never know exactly what was said, and we've all had a laugh about it, but let's be mindful not to make Mike Dean out to be some sort of hero now.

Abou Diaby announced his retirement from football this week, a timely reminder of just how bad a referee Mike Dean is.

Some of his behaviour has actually almost taken some of the focus off of just how atrocious this helmet is at his job, and made him into some kind of cult. The reality, of course, is that he is something quite similar sounding to "cult."

Wednesday February 27th, 2019
Arsenal 5 AFC Bournemouth 1

Now, this is more like it. This is the kind of result and performance that makes watching Match of the Day, and Alan Shearer's shiny, bald peanut head in midweek a pleasure, rather than a chore.

Once again, we got an early goal, and I can't help thinking how important it is for this team to start well. Hardly rocket science, I know, but it was all well and good having a laugh about "Second Half Arsenal FC" while we were on a winning run earlier in the season, I'm pretty sure that it started having a detrimental, psychological effect once the run came to an end.

The early goal tonight came from Ozil, who finished with a skill that only Ozil can pull off and has now come to be known as "The Ozil." You know what that is by now; the way that he somehow manages to hit the ball into the ground.

He even boasted about "The Ozil" with his goal celebration. This looked a lot better than when Olivier Giroud did a "scorpion kick" celebration against Bournemouth that time and ended up looking like Eric Morecambe. I'm a big fan of the potential comedic value of a player celebrates a goal reflecting the way he scores, though.

It would have been great watching Frank Lampard a few years ago, somehow running into a defender and deflecting his celebration off of them. Ozil was then involved in the second as he teed the ball up nicely for Mkhitaryan. Of course, we usually need to "Arsenal" at least once in most games these days, and this week's Arsenaller was Guendouzi, as he was caught Arsenalling around on the edge of the box, and our lead was halved.

Thankfully, this seemed to remind the visitors that they're called "AFC" Bournemouth, and as they decided to pretty much stop bothering to try and defend after half-time. Once Koscielny got our third just a minute into the second half, that was that, and Lacabameyang helped put a couple of plus points on the goal difference. With Auba having been substituted, Ozil proved he's a man of many talents by taking his place in the little handshake celebration thing. Laca doesn't strike me as the jealous type but maybe Mesut ought to watch his back in training this week, just in case.

It was great to see Unai maintaining his intensity on the touchline even if at times it looked as though we were playing against the Dog and Duck Second XI in the second half. Fair play to him.

Three wins on the bounce within a week, conceding just the one goal. Could this be the start of another run, is this New New New Arsenal?

God only knows with us, but I tell you what; if it is, then it could well be a season defining one. Our next three games are that lot at their foster home, Rennes away in the Thursday-night-stupid-o'clock-kick-off-league, then United at home. Get something decent out of those, and maybe we can begin to believe once more that we might get at least something from this season.

With them losing at Chelsea tonight as well, this time it's us with the momentum going into the NLD. As nice as that is, what with this fixture being what it is - and Arsenal being Arsenal – somehow it doesn't necessarily give you the confidence you'd expect it to. Welcome back to The North London Derby, ladies and gentlemen; a truly unique experience.

Saturday March 2nd, 2019
Tottenham Hotspur 1 Arsenal 1
Right, you don't need me to tell you how frustrating today was do you? A lot has come out of this game, so I'll attempt to break it

down as I have a feeling it's going to take us all the way through to the first leg against Rennes on Thursday.

If there is one good thing to come from football supporters' lives being in the hands of the television companies, it's when this particular fixture kicks off at 12.30. The NLD nerves are almost impossible to supress, but the less time you have to think about it, the better. As I said, I had been lucky enough to keep a lid on things during the week due to what was going on in real-life, and I also managed to keep myself occupied enough during the morning of the game. I didn't even go out to get beer until around twenty minutes before kick-off. In hindsight, I'm not so sure that any of this was a good idea, as from that moment on the delayed reaction had me just as on edge as I would have been if I'd spent the whole week watching the "Spurs Victories Over Arsenal" DVD. Fucks sake.

Having managed to avoid any mention of the game up until then, the Arsenal line-up had me shitting bricks as well, not least Mustafi at right-back. Thank you, Unai!

Kick-off time, and we didn't start too badly. There was clearly a game plan and we looked like we were sticking to it. This appeared to be compounded when Aaron Ramsey was sent clear to put us in front inside twenty minutes. His celebration, glaring at the Spurs fans whilst proclaiming "this is my fucking ground" was as saddening as it was exhilarating, as the realisation dawned that after giving us some of the best memories in recent years at this stadium, we wouldn't see him there again after today.

Not too much time to dwell on that thought though. Well, actually there was plenty of time to dwell on it, as the game seemed to go on for so long after the goal that I had to keep checking outside to see if it had gotten dark.

NLD nerves are a genuine phenomenon. Somehow, you are more nervous at 1-0 than you are at 0-0. In fact, I would say there's even a chance that you're more nervous at 1-0 up than you are at 1-0 down!

It's a feeling that's impossible to actually put into words, but for some reason when we are 1-0 up, I automatically assume that at some point we are going to be 2-1 down.

Nothing was helping these nerves either, especially the uneasy feeling coming from Mcmananamanamanamanaman giving Spurs the sort of stick he usually reserves for us. This must be what it feels like not being an Arsenal fan!

Around seven hours later, they were awarded a penalty and the rest, as they say, is history. Let's not piss about here; Harry Kane was offside. If you have any doubt about it, consider this; Harry Kane was offside enough for Steve McManaman to say, when the penalty was awarded – and before a replay was shown – that he thought Harry Kane was offside. Steve McManaman. Mind you, he also thought that Danny Rose "had to go for the ball", when what he actually did was go for the ball, miss it, then follow through with his studs up into Leno's chest, so spotting an offside doesn't really make him any less of an arsehole.

Again, I have no doubt whatsoever that the fallout from this will last long into next week (and possibly beyond), and you will have had enough of it by then, let alone by the time you get to read this, so I'll sum the rest of the game up as briefly as possible.

We were awarded what could be described as a "soft" penalty (still onside, though), which was saved by Lloris. Iwobi then squared the follow up back to Auba, but Jan Vertonghen blocked what looked as if it would be a tap-in on the line. "Macca and Fletch" were so busy touching themselves (and possibly each other) over that, that they failed to pick up the fact that Vertonghen had encroached so far into the box before the penalty was taken that he may as well have taken the fucking thing himself.

Game over, but not before Torreira was shown a straight red for a challenge on Danny Rose that was no worse than the one Rose put in on Leno and didn't even get booked for.

I'm sure it isn't just me, but I get the distinct feeling that there is going to be a lot of complete and utter bollocks spoken in the coming days....

Yeah, it didn't take long at all for the "journalists" to start bending over backwards to find reasons as to why the foul on Sir Harry Kane being given was the correct decision. In fact, it only took until 23.19pm on Saturday night, as Sam Wallace from The Independent tweeted this:

"Have sought expert opinion on the Kane penalty. Consensus is that while his offside position occurs first, the offside offence comes after Mustafi foul. In eyes of officials (although not MOTD)

Kane not yet playing or attempting to play ball when fouled. Correct decision."

He attached an image to the tweet – a screenshot from the FA website – with a paragraph circled, apparently proving his point. What he seemed to miss, though, was the paragraph directly below it, which made his proclamation of "correct decision" appear to be complete horseshit. I'm not going to quote either paragraph here, you've probably seen it already anyway. What I will mention is the fact that Alan Shearer engaged in a conversation with him in the replies, and Alan Shearer made more sense. Let's rewind a bit there. Steve McManaman and Alan Shearer have come out of this situation looking sensible. Makes you think, doesn't it?

Let's rewind a bit further than that though, to Wallace's tweet.

Firstly; "Have sought expert opinion on the Kane penalty..." for fucks sake turn it in, Sam, it's 23.19pm on a Saturday night, mate. Have a look for something to watch on Netflix or something.

Even if you ignore that, you could consider this; the offence took place before two o'clock this afternoon, meaning it's taken this pillock about nine hours to come to this conclusion. Does he (or anyone) honestly think that the linesman, in that split second, suddenly thought to himself "Hang on... law 11, section 3 states that a player in an offside position is moving towards the ball with the intention of playing the ball and is fouled before playing or attempting to play the ball, or challenging an opponent for the ball, the foul is penalised as it has occurred before the offside offence... so I won't put my flag up..." ? Bollocks.

This might just be the slightest bit believable if he was even level with play, as he should have been, but he wasn't. Let's be honest here, the linesman missed the offside, that's why the penalty was given. Sam Wallace can sit there Saturday night seeking "expert opinion" (a PDF of the offside law, to be precise) all he wants, and he'll not find a more valid explanation than that.

With all of this, people's thoughts inevitably turned to VAR. This is a debate that will go on for.... well ... forever, probably. As will next season at this rate. You can't keep people happy as it is, so the only way VAR can possibly work is to use it for every decision in every game. I hope you're looking forward to my next book – "VAR – Life as an Arsenal fan, 2019/29"!

Week Thirty March 3rd – 9th, 2019
Spursy and Arsenally

You may have noticed this, but when things such as the fallout from the weekend start to drag on for days, I get bored of them quite quickly. Sometimes there is a particular moment which leads me to go... "Whoah... that's enough of that, thank you!"

On this occasion, that moment came courtesy of Danny Rose proclaiming that Pochettino's half-time team talk as "one of the best things I have witnessed in football" and that "it was like he was really sending us to war." I had a quick look at Danny Rose's Wikipedia page, and the "Honours" section reads thusly:

Tottenham Hotspur
• Football League Cup runner-up: 2014–15
England
• FIFA World Cup fourth place: 2018
Individual
• Sunderland Young Player of the Season: 2012–13
• PFA Team of the Year: 2015–16 Premier League, 2016–17 Premier League

On the face of it, the greatest achievement of Danny Rose's career so far, is a League Cup runners-up medal. The very definition of Spursy.

If you take that into consideration, it is quite easy to believe that a half-time team talk that led to Tottenham getting a draw due to the complete incompetence of Premier League match officials, and a penalty missed in injury-time, is indeed one of the best things that Danny Rose has witnessed in football.

I must say I'm particularly impressed by the inclusion of the PFA teams of the year in his list of honours. I wouldn't be surprised if he's put that one in there himself.

Like, "yeah, but what have you done in your career?"

"Erm... HELLOOOO! I was in the PFA team of the year for two seasons in a row thank you very much!" Spursy.

Elsewhere, journalists were of course bending over backwards to praise "Poch" for his "war cry" that could "revive their season" or some load of old bollocks like that.

Dinnertime with Sam Wallace is a fascinating affair, as he demonstrates his own version of the offside law with condiments, sauces and various kitchen utensils. Yeah, this all got boring very quickly.

I decided to try and make it fun by imaging a parallel universe in which Aubameyang had actually scored from the spot. In this parallel universe, nobody has heard a peep from the Sunderland Young Player of the Season 2012-13 all week, and various journalists are analysing footage of the penalty incident frame-by-frame to prove beyond reasonable doubt that the decision to award the penalty to Arsenal was wrong.

The novelty wore off once I realised that I was actually beginning to get irritated by a universe that didn't even exist. Thoughts then turned to the next in a series of important fixtures, the last 16, first-leg against Rennes.

Thursday March 7th, 2019
Rennes 3 Arsenal 1

We've seen this happen a lot over the years, but off the top of my head I think this is the most "Arsenally" performance I can remember for a while. We couldn't have gotten off to a better start, with good fortune playing its part in Iwobi opening the scoring, as he put a ball into the box that evaded everyone and crept in off of the post.

On 42 minutes, Arsenal decided it was time to Arsenal. Sokratis was sent off for a second yellow, after what was a daft challenge considering he had already been booked. The resulting free-kick was played into the wall, but the rebound was fired in like an absolute rocket.

We've seen this movie before, so I might as well keep it brief. True to form, things went steadily downhill after that, and the home side's lead was doubled through a Monreal own-goal. 1-0 up before the Six O'clock News, 2-1 down halfway through Eastenders.

Arsenally.

On 88 minutes came a real hammer blow, when we were caught on the break, with Guendouzi, deciding that this would be a good time to forget about running about a lot, channelling his inner Denilson and have a little jog back instead.

Not an impossible position to come back from by any means, but we are left with it all to do in the home leg.

If we do need any extra motivation, then it comes in the form of Hatem Ben Arfa being a bit of a twat.

"My motivation was to play a solid match, to win and get ourselves into a good position to go through," Wow. Revolutionary stuff there, mate.

"That's what was in my head. But I did see the same Emery, as agitated as ever. I looked over at him a few times and that made me laugh a little. He hasn't changed."

"I told some friends before the match that my prediction was that we would win 3-1 or 4-1. We didn't manage to get the fourth, but my prediction was right."

Let's hope we can make him eat his words this time next week. Not that he looks shy of a meal or two, mind.

This week has left me rather confused and conflicted, if I'm honest. Although the result of the NLD may have been disappointing, I saw the kind of positives in the performance that I don't think I've seen for a few months. Not sure I can really put my finger on it, it's just a feeling I had. Plus, there looked like there was a firm game-plan that, for the main part, we stuck to.

Just as I started to wonder if maybe, just maybe, we were starting to turn a corner again, we go and pull an absolute Arsenal, in France. Two games that were completely different but left me feeling equally frustrated for completely different reasons.

This is Arsenal.

This is Arsenally.

If nothing else, at least if this is how Emery is going to carry on, he's certainly at the right club!

Week Thirty-One
March 10th – 16th, 2019
Murder on the Dancefloor, Unai's at the Wheel

As I said before the Tottenham game, this could well be a season defining period. Recent results around us mean that we are now in a genuine battle for fourth place. As frustrating as that Tottenham result was, I still took some confidence from it, as despite whatever nonsense was written about "war cries" and what have you, we were a missed penalty and a slow linesman away from taking three points away from Wembley and being right up their backsides. They were lucky. They know they were.

Today we face United at home, which is massive. Get three points today and it really is game on.

Sunday March 10th, 2019
Arsenal 2 Manchester United 0

Arsenal dragged English football into the gutter today, with a disgraceful 2-0 victory over Manchester United. Unai Emery's men showed a blatant disregard for narrative in beating poor little Ole Gunnar's men, reducing grown men to tears in the process.

Gary Neville spent ninety minutes as that Gary Neville, rather than the one we've all reluctantly taken to as a Sky Sports pundit.

Brother Philip was later seeing crying into a visibly upset Alan Shearer's lap on Match of the Day 2.

"United could easily have won that 3-0" he sobbed, seemingly oblivious to the fact that it is impossible to beat a team 3-0 that has scored two goals against you.

How satisfying was this result? There was steam coming out of people's ears by the end of this.

Graeme Souness is the one that confuses me a bit. He clearly hates Arsenal. He's also an ex-Liverpool man though, so you would expect him to be happy to see United get beat.

The only conclusion one can come to is that he is suffering from what is known as John Aldridge Syndrome, an affliction that can affect anyone that has been associated with Liverpool Football club, and the symptoms of which include waking up in the middle of the night screaming "SMITH NEVER TOUCHED THE BALL, REF!"

I must admit I barely listen to a word this idiot says these days, but what I did catch was him criticising Aubameyang's penalty. Which he scored. "It's not even a good penalty" or something like that.

Okay, mate, we'll strike that one off because of poor technique, shall we?

A good penalty is when the football goes into the goal, a not good penalty is when the football does not go into the goal, Graeme.

As for the game itself, I thought it was a great performance from us despite what anyone else outside of Arsenal might tell you. The reaction to Xhaka's goal was absolutely hilarious.

Okay, I think it's fair to say that he didn't exactly intend for the ball to move in the manner that he did, but the way the Sky commentary team were falling over themselves to deny him any credit whatsoever – and put it down to a goalkeeping error from De Gea - was highly amusing. How many times have they criticised us for not shooting from outside the box over the years?!

Plus, when you think of how often De Gea has had an absolute blinder against us, I honestly couldn't give a toss whether it was his fault, or that Xhaka has secretly created some new way of making the ball move after it's left his boot, like in some Playstation game or something.

United had plenty of the game, as well as a number of good chances, but found Leno in better form than his opposite number.

On 68 minutes, we were awarded a penalty when Laca was bundled over in the box, and up stepped his other half, Auba to banish his demons from missing against that lot and double our lead. Fair play to him for stepping up, and even fairer play to him for rolling it down the middle (consequently causing Souness' head to explode), after the other week. If that had been me, I would have absolutely twatted it. Which is why I'm sitting here writing this in my pants rather than taking penalties for The Arsenal.

My personal favourite moment of the match, however, came around ten minutes later, when Kolasinac chucked his guts up on the pitch. Brought back memories of Hackney Marshes back in the day, did that.

A very satisfying result going into the second leg against Rennes on Thursday, and not a moonwalking dickhead on the Emirates pitch in sight today. What was that about the perils of over-celebrating? "The Emirates is our dancefloor" indeed.

Big shout to Mr Emery as well. I've been critical of him lately, not entirely without reason as far as I'm concerned either. I mean, it is possible to question whether the man in charge is the right man for the job without "calling for his head" is it not?

The problem is that it's nigh-on impossible to have an opinion on anything these days without being pigeonholed. Well, I'm staying firmly out of any pigeon's hole by contradicting myself on a weekly basis at the moment, thank you very much.

This week, I am very much pro-Emery. The team selection against United was bolder than I'm sure a lot of us were expecting, and it paid off.

Turn the Europa tie around on Thursday, and I might even invite him round for dinner!

I've always found the aftermath of a victory like that almost as good as the result itself, so I very much enjoyed the next few days spent basking in that victory, with everyone fuming at the fact that we had ruined their little "Ole's at the wheel" party.

Not too much time to sit back and pat ourselves on the back, however, as there is the small matter of trying to overturn a two-goal deficit against Rennes on Thursday.

Thursday March 14th, 2019
Arsenal 3 Rennes 0

A few weeks ago, I said that the good thing about being beaten by a tractor firm was that at least it got everyone up for the Europa League once more. Well, that's the case again this week, after we went and Arsenalled the first leg.

There are plenty of rallying cries out there this week... "Let's fill the place up!" tweets, accompanied by a screenshot of how many seats are still available in the ground. Absolutely right as well. We are getting towards the business end of the season now, and there is plenty to play for.

Sunday's shameful win over United has galvanised us Arsenal supporters, as much as it angered the rest of the country. That's just how we like it, ain't it?

Tonight, is the last Arsenal action for almost three weeks. How nice would it be to go into the break by going through to the quarter finals of the Europa League, just a few days after making the Neville brothers cry?

A 2-0 win will take us through, but I'm not sure our collective underwear will survive should we go anywhere past 80 minutes only 2-0 up. I'll happily take being 84-0 up by half-time just to settle the nerves, like.

We got off to the best possible start, with Aubameyang putting us ahead on five minutes. Ten minutes later, it was advantage Arsenal as Maitland-Niles doubled our lead in hilariously controversial fashion. Aubameyang was offside when he crossed for young AMN to head home, which BT Sport spent more time trying to prove than they obviously did interviewing for the co-commentary roles.

("So, Mr Robson, do you have any previous experience?"

"Well, I managed to get myself sacked from Arsenal TV, for wild criticism of the actual Arsenal manager."

"Can you work Thursday nights?"

"I can work any night. I'll work every night if you like. For free. I don't have many friends you see, and..."

"Congratulations, Mr Robson, you've got the job....")

This must have been like porn for Sam Wallace.

That obviously boiled the piss of the Rennes players somewhat, and the game got quite "niggly" after that. I don't like niggly. Especially with a cup-tie so precariously perched as this one. That's when "niggly" becomes "nervy", and "nervy" is never an enjoyable way to watch a football match. "Niggly" + "Nervy" = a strong chance of "Arsenalling", in my experience.

If that goal boiled Rennes piss, then Aubameyang's celebration after scoring our third, and ultimately sealing the tie, caused an absolute tsunami of hot, steamy urine, as he ran behind the goal, and pulled out a Black Panther mask, put it on, and did the "Wakanda Forever" thing. Oh, mate, this is going to be fun in the morning.

Having said that, he would have looked a proper knob had we not won the game, let's be honest. He actually did his best to balls it up for us after that, missing two sitters along the way.

As it was, we did win the game, and I look forward to waking up in a sea of gloriously boiling piss in the morning. (Not literally. That's not happened for a while now.)

The only disappointment was Emery not running up to Ben Arfa and waving his willy in his face. Ben Arfa? J Arthur, more like! (Ask your parents, kids...) As predicted, the next morning was indeed a sea of boiling social media piss.

Even some Arsenal fans were "embarrassed" by it. Don't get me wrong, I get where this point of view is coming from; we'd be ripping the arse out of Harry Kane if he had done it (*insert "doesn't he wear a mask every game joke here*), but at the end of the day; that's how it works isn't it?

I would have been embarrassed if we hadn't won the game, but we did, and Arsenal winning football matches annoys lots of people, so let's not get annoyed about a fucking mask ourselves, eh?

Plus, having been an Arsenal supporter for over four decades now, I've suffered waaaay more embarrassment than a geezer in a panther mask, mate.

So, after a bit of a dodgy spell, throughout which I must admit I was beginning to have serious doubts about the manager (but that's one for another day), we are in great form going into the business end of the season.

Once again, if we look back to the beginning of the season, we would have been well happy with being in a genuine battle for top four, and still in the Europa League had you offered it to us back then.

Perhaps my doubts about the manager will resurface should we fail in any of those objectives, I really don't know at the moment.

What I do know is, with Unai at the Wheel... it's gonna be a wild ride. I'm happy with that after how tragically uninteresting things had gotten last season. Hold on tight!

Week Thirty-Two
March 17th – (what feels like the) 300th, 2019
Boooooooorrrrrring!!!

No Arsenal action for a whole fortnight. From a footballing point of view, it's come at a kind of frustrating time seeing as we were building a nice bit of momentum. From a fans point of view, it's great going into the break on a high because if nothing else at least it means we don't have a lot to argue about. Anyone that has spent time as an Arsenal fan during this social media age will know just what a joy it would have been if we had lost to United and / or Rennes.

This, the first of three weekends without Arsenal, is FA Cup weekend. As far as I'm concerned, this is the greatest club cup competition on Earth... until Arsenal aren't in it any more. Once we're out it might as well be the Carabao Cup; that's how much of a shit I give about it. It's the quarter-finals this weekend, and such was my disinterest that I didn't even know Watford were still in it until we came out of Watford station last night, on our way to see friends, and saw a few Watford fans singing about "goin' to Wemberlee."

"Oh, Watford must've won then..."

Incidentally, I've just used the word "Watford" four times in one paragraph. I feel like I should break out into a chorus of Rocket Man in a minute.

Bloody hell, it's gonna be a long couple of weeks ain't it...

So, all quiet on the Arsenal front this week, and a relatively calm, happy and united fanbase. If only there were something else to pass the time. If only there were something that is causing a huge divide, ruining friendships, and being a source of hyperbole, overreaction and mass social media propaganda, eh?

We are currently living in a world where it has become normal to label people as "Remainers" and "Brexiteers." Honestly, read that back again. "Remainers" and "Brexiteers." Deary me.

Don't worry, I'm not gonna start getting all political. I don't really "do" politics, but surely, I can't be the only person to notice the parallels between Brexit and "Wexit"? (Yes, there were people that seriously used that term last year, without the slightest hint of irony!)

Remainers vs Brexiteers. AKB vs WOB.

Spend a few days on Twitter over this next couple of weeks and tell me that you can't see the parallels between the two.

It's quite amusing, and one thing that has struck me most as a similarity, is that some people seem to actually love it, in the same way that some people seemed to love the Wenger Wars.

Anyway, as it's an Arsenal break, I think it's time for another one of those little interludes isn't it? Funnily enough, this is an international break. So on that note...

CLUB VERSUS COUNTRY

Friday night we have the other reason for our enforced Arsenal break – the Euro 2020 qualifiers. I find it difficult to get myself motivated for internationals other than the actual tournaments themselves, if I'm honest. However, I'm certainly not one of those that like to go on about how boring international football is, and I have nothing but admiration for those that follow their national team around the world.

Oddly, supporting England during a tournament comes with its own problems as well.

I threw myself fully behind England during the World Cup, on the back of a painful and turbulent season at Arsenal, and I thought nothing of it at all. I mean; that's normal, right? The sun was out, the beer was flowing, it was even the perfect excuse for... erm... not working as hard as one might do.

Well, according to some, that wasn't right because of the number of Tottenham players in the England squad.

"Can't believe you're cheering Harry Kane and Dele Alli on... you've been slagging him off all season... blah, blah..."

Yes, because that's how it works, you miserable bastards.

Don't get me wrong, I do get where that point of view comes from, and if I'm honest I'd probably be lying if I said I don't feel a little dirty afterwards (usually after sobering up), but as far as I'm concerned; I'm "cheering on" Harry Kane the England player, not Harry Kane the Tottenham player. They're a different player when they put the Tottenham shirt on. Hell, they're a different fucking species when they've got that shirt on.

I don't even feel that I'm "cheering on" the player as an individual, more the England team as a collective.

If you find that hypocritical... well, you'd be right, but you'd also be forgetting the fact that, as I have mentioned a few times already, hypocrisy is one of the many rights afforded to us football supporters, so do me a favour, pal; fuck off and watch the cricket for a month if it bothers you that much.

It never used to be like this, did it?

I remember growing up watching Glenn Hoddle and I can't really remember it bothering me that he was one of them when he was playing for England.

Perhaps there just weren't as many wankers in English football back then. Or maybe I just didn't realise they were wankers. I mean, if you were to ask me now what I think of Glenn Hoddle, there's a good chance I would answer "he's a wanker, that Glenn Hoddle", to be honest.

Speaking of which; if you think it's bad with the current crop we have playing for England; cast your mind back a few years and imagine how bad it was having to support a team that had Teddy Sheringham in it. Now, there's a proper... ehem!

I'm not sure exactly what the main reason was for people to suddenly decide that it's not okay to support your own country anymore, but I guess it began with the influx of overseas players into the English game. The fewer English players at your club, the less chance there is of having any of them in the England squad.

The intensity of the competition in the Premier League is another factor, although it's not as if that tribal element hasn't always been there. In fact, that element was even more prominent years ago, it's just that the modern football supporter finds it hard to separate club level tribalism to the international game. As in; it's okay to hate each other every week when there isn't an international game on.

In summary, the club vs country thing is just another in a long line of pointless fucking arguments that are arguments for the sake of arguing. This, my friends, is not only modern football in a nutshell; it's modern life in a nutshell. Here endeth the lesson.

Week 33
April 1st - 7th, 2019
The Return of St Totteringham's Day?

A few weeks ago, it seemed highly unlikely that we would finish above Tottenham. Even finishing in the top four seemed quite a stretch.

Today, we sit just a point behind them in fifth, with a game in hand, meaning that St. Totteringham's Day is now in our hands, and a win - or at least a draw - at home to Newcastle would see us move above them into third for a couple of days at least.

Let's not kid ourselves, history tells us that there is every chance we will still balls this up, so it's probably not a good idea to get our hopes up too much just yet.

It's impossible, however, not to quietly consider just how hilarious it would be for this to happen, as well as the possibility of the new footballing superpower to finish outside of the top four.

Yeah, there's still a lot of football to be played, but the sight of Tim Sherwood cacking his pants on Match of the Day as he contemplated this scenario was a sight to behold. I genuinely thought he might start blubbing at one point.

One can only imagine the state he will be in, should St Totteringham's Day return this year. The mind boggles.

Anyway, let's put Tim Sherwood and his weird little world to one side for a minute, and concentrate on the real world.

There is a real buzz about tonight. A nervous energy. We've all been laughing at the North London Superpower after yesterday's last-minute capitulation, but now, our collective arses are beginning to twitch a bit. Fair play for you that have been bold enough to tweet "we're going third tonight" and such, but you'll see no such thing from me.

I have no problem with laughing at that lot, after their, quite frankly hilarious, last-minute loss to Liverpool yesterday, though.

I've never been an advocate of the "let's win our game before we laugh at them" theory. You need to get as many laughs in as possible as an Arsenal fan these days, and if we were to Arsenal this up tonight, it doesn't necessarily make them Spursing it yesterday any less amusing, does it? On to the game, then.

Monday April 1st, 2019
Arsenal 2 Newcastle 0

Well, well, well. Who'd have thought it? We never even looked like Arsenalling this one up at all. Despite Anthony Taylor's efforts, that is.

Arsene Wenger once famously told Taylor he was "dishonest to his federation." I don't think anyone can argue with that, unless of course Anthony Taylor belongs to the Federation of Useless Twats. Arsene also told Taylor to "fuck off." I don't think anyone can argue with that either.

That's now ten home wins in a row, which is something I must admit I was not aware of until it was mentioned. I would say that's down to the fact that we have been quietly going about our business, while the mainstream media masturbate themselves into a frenzy, fighting amongst themselves over who will be the first one to give #SpursNewStadium a creampie.

Anthony Taylor began his stirring performance as Anthony Taylor, in The Man Who Was Dishonest to His Federation, early on, disallowing Ramsey's goal for pretty much no reason at all. There was a slight foul in the box as the ball made its way to Ramsey, maybe, but I don't think it affected the finish from Ramsey at all.

There was no such nonsense when Ramsey put us ahead on the half hour mark, however. In your face, Mr Dishonest!

Despite our dominance, we had to wait until the 84th minute to be sure of the three points, with a lovely finish from Laca, put through by 'Bameyang, putting the game to bed.

In all honesty, we could have had five or six. There were some great perfomances out there as well, with Ramsey, Lacazette and Ozil outstanding. Ozil's performance was one of those that had you wishing we saw more of that from him. At times unplayable.

Young Guendouzi was the subject of the Arsenal fans debate the next day, and he seems to have joined Iwobi in the "is he shit?" club. I'm not quite as sold on him yet as some people are, but he is young, and having some from the depths of the French second division, or whatever, into a team such as ours, and probably playing a lot more than we (or even he!) expected, I think he deserves both our credit and our patience.

In summary; he has been neither as bad or as good as he's been labelled by us fans this season, and there has been some going over the top on both "sides." Business as usual, then! We could probably have signed Pele in his pomp and some of our fans would have labelled him a flop. If you'll pardon the pun.

So, we go above the mighty Tottenham Hotspur - and their really long bar - until they no doubt beat Palace at home on Wednesday.

As can be expected, on the day of that game, the new stadium is all that everyone is going on about. Everyone is at it with this comparison to the Emirates as well, with even William Hill joining in on Twitter. This whole situation really is the perfect example of using clickbait to hook Arsenal fans, but it's also getting a bit fucking weird now. They won, of course. The Footballing Gods were never going to be that kind to us, were they?

The opening ceremony at the Stadium of Lifts, was quite something. An operatic version of Glory Glory Tottenham Hotspur, with accompanying fireworks was the moment it was transformed from a massive wankfest to a complete cringefest.

I've spoken about that lot way too much lately, to the point that some wally on Twitter would tell me that I'm "obsessed", or "triggered", or some shite like that. That's not the case as far as I'm concerned, though. Football supporters have been "obsessed" with their local rivals for years now, it's how the game works. Also, if we're going to talk about who's obsessed, try looking for tweets on the new stadium, and see how many times Arsenal or the Emirates are mentioned alongside it as a means of comparison.

I'm planning a little bonus chapter on this comparison in a couple of weeks, so I will leave you with this... Spending a billion quid on a stadium with 32 lifts, seven escalators, 4,155 steps, 60 food and drink outlets and 1,800 HD screens, then getting the bloke off the Go Compare ads to open it, is the most Tottenham Hotspur thing that Tottenham Hotspur have ever done.

Week 34
April 7th - 13th, 2019
Aaron Ramsey Punched My Cat

A big few weeks ahead of us. Top four is now in our hands, and we have a two-legged Europa League quarter final tie with Napoli. This means we are challenging to return to the Champions League on two fronts! (I wonder if they'll let us in it twice next season?) Hold on tight!

Sunday April 7th, 2019
Everton 1 Arsenal 0

If there's one thing in our lives that is consistent, it's Arsenal's capacity to bring us crashing down to earth just as we are getting our hopes up. After a couple of weeks where the optimism came flowing back, everything is shit again.

During his little mini-meltdown the other week, Tim Sherwood said that he can see Arsenal winning every game for the rest of the season, and I believed him. My hopes had been raised to the point that I believed that Tim Sherwood might be talking sense.

The last couple of weeks had given me so much hope that I had actually completely forgotten about how shit we are away from home.

I had forgotten how shit we are at defending. I had forgotten just how collectively shit we can be at football.

At least nobody can fault our commitment to that particular cause. We were beaten by a goal scored by 78-year-old Phil Jagielka.

Jagielka once went in goal against Arsenal - for Sheffield United after their keeper, Paddy Kenny, went off injured with United leading 1-0 - and, against a team including Robin Van Persie, kept a clean sheet. That's real dedication to the cause from us. Make no mistake, 1-0 flattered us. Everton could have had four or five today.

If it wasn't for our capacity to massively let ourselves down just when it matters most, I would be happy to join the "it's only one game FFS.... stop the negativity FFS...." camp. As it is, I'm not really feeling that at the moment. We have four more away games to play – Watford, Wolves, Leicester and Burnley, and in all honesty, I can see us not winning any of them. This isn't some sort of reverse psychology nonsense either. I can genuinely see us doing what will come to be known as a "Reverse Tim Sherwood."

There really isn't much to say about his game other than we were totally awful. Probably the worst we've been since West Ham away. The players should have a word with themselves, but so should the manager, I'm afraid.

Seeing a starting lineup that includes Elneny and Guendouzi in midfield... well, let's just say that the outcome of the game was exactly what most of us thought it would be. Aaron Ramsey was on the bench and apparently, he had been carrying a knock. I would go as far as to say that you could amputate both of Aaron Ramsey's legs and he would be more effective than that pair together. Don't get me wrong, I like Elneny, you're always guaranteed to get 100% from him, I just think 10% of Ramsey is more suited to Everton away than 100% of Elneny is. Harsh, maybe, but I don't mean it to be, it is what it is. Plus, he's off to Italy at the end of the season, not sure I give a toss if we play him until his legs fall off until then.

It's quite funny (well, no it's not really) how quickly we can go from "that's it, we're above Tottenham, we'll win every game now", to "oh shit, I totally forgot how pony we can be away from home, we're screwed ain't we?"

The mood among the fanbase in the wake of the Everton game has certainly reflected that, as the focus has switched to hilarious "Arsenal Home vs Arsenal Away" tweets. Can't say I blame anyone for feeling that way, it's there for all to see.

Thankfully, we also have a huge game to focus on; namely Napoli at home in the Europa League quarter-finals on Thursday.

The fact that the first leg is at home has worked in our favour this time, in my opinion. We really could do without playing away again this week!

Thursday April 11th, 2019
Arsenal 2 Napoli 0

Imagine that. You play your strongest team available to you, and this happens. Much the same as the 1-0 defeat at Everton didn't reflect their superiority, this scoreline doesn't do our performance justice either. If that's not a reflection on the difference in our home and away form, then I don't know what is. It certainly reflects it more than a few amusing tweets does!

We got off to a superb start, and it wasn't long before we were ahead, Aaron Ramsey finishing off a superb, sweeping move. Eleven minutes later, it was 2-0 as Torreira's shot was deflected off of Koulibaly. I actually felt sorry for Koulibaly because, from the moment Ian Darke (didn't he used to do the boxing?) and Robbie Savage started sucking him off, he suddenly became Igor Stepanovs.

Speaking of Robbie Savage; there seems to be something strange going on there. Now, this is going completely against the grain as far as this whole book goes, but he's starting to, erm... talk sense every now and then.

It's getting to the point where I'm starting to agree with him from time to time, and it's quite an uncomfortable feeling, to be honest. There was a time when he would spout the usual BT Sport sponsored anti-Arsenal bollocks for ninety minutes non-stop, but he seems to have eased up on that now, and I'm even starting to wonder whether an Arsenal fan has got something on him, and he's being blackmailed.

Mind you, having seen the state of him on Strictly Come Dancing, it's hard to imagine anyone having any worse on him than that isn't it? The mind boggles.

I want to hate Aaron Ramsey. I want him to be absolute crap for the rest of the season. I want him to cost us a place in the top four. I want him to miss an open goal on purpose in the last seconds of injury time in the Europa League final, then proceed to miss the penalty in the resulting shootout that hands the trophy to the opposition. Not just miss it, but REALLY miss it. In fact, I want him to start his run up from the halfway line, then when he reaches the ball, to kick it in the opposite direction to the goal, then tear off his Arsenal shirt to reveal a Tottenham one underneath, and to celebrate with the opposition players.

I want Aaron Ramsey to punch my cat.

I want all of this, because at the moment, it seems less painful than watching him leave Arsenal.

For the record, I had prepared myself for him leaving a while ago (at least, I thought I had), and him leaving to go abroad at the end of this contract was, in my opinion, always going to happen. He was outstanding tonight. The bastard.

It's amazing to think that the "is Iwobi shit?" and "is Guendouzi shit?" movements were originally the "Aaron Ramsey is shit" movement.

Of course, there are still a few stragglers left over, and they have formed the "Ramsey isn't really that good. He was good for a few months back in 2014/15, but he's been too inconsistent. Yeah, maybe he has scored winners in two FA Cup Finals, but no way does that make him a legend" club. Or, to give it it's rightful name; the "I slagged Ramsey off to the point of no return a few years ago, and I am now unable to say anything nice about him without looking a bit of a tit" club.

For now, I suppose the best thing to do is enjoy him while he's still here. Enjoy him through the haze of bitter tears. The cat-punching little bastard.

All in all, I guess we need to at least try and force ourselves to be happy with taking a 2-0 lead to Napoli next week. It could have been better; we could genuinely have scored 4 or 5, but on the other hand, it could have been a lot worse too, because they also had their chances. If you look back to the semi-final first leg against Atletico last season; we could have had one foot in the final by half-time, but instead made a complete and utter Arsenal of it and gifted them the away goal. For that reason, and because I have been leaning way more towards the negative side of the fence than I would like to lately, I'm going to place myself fully in the "a 2-0 win against Napoli in the quarter-finals of the Europa League is a good result" camp. It all looks a lot more obvious when you put it that way doesn't it?

The mood among the fanbase for the next few days is one of cautious optimism. Every game is massive from now on until the end of the season, which is how we want it, isn't it? The irony in the fact that being in a battle for top 4 was what we wanted this season, after so many years of mocking it, isn't lost on me, but that doesn't matter right now. It doesn't matter, because for the last two seasons, we weren't even in that battle!

Plus, if we look way back to the beginning of the season, we would all have given our private parts to be in a position to get our arses back in the Champions League, so challenging for that on two fronts – one of which would result in our first European trophy for many a year – well, it beats spending the next month praying for the season to end!

Week 35
April 14th - 20th, 2019
Entering the Business End

Well, this is it, people. This is officially, well and truly what is known as "the business end of the season." What does this mean? Well, Collins English Dictionary defines the business end thusly: "The part of a tool or weapon that does the work, as contrasted with the handle...."

For example; "never pick up a knife by the business end", or "I would love to smash Teddy Sheringham across his stupid face with the business end of a shovel...." That kind of thing.

In football terms, the "business end of the season" is when shit gets real. It's when title battles are decided. When relegation battles are decided.

When the Premier League Team of the Year is decided, sparking huge social media debate (HOW IS *insert player of hated rivals here* IN THE TEAM AND *insert player that plays in the same position for the team you support here* NOT FFS!!!!!!!!!!!!) When the winners are separated from the also rans. That kind of thing. It's make or break time.

In Arsenal terms, the business end of the season, 2019, is when we are battling with Chelsea, Man United and, to a lesser extent, Tottenham, for "Who is Going to Make the Biggest Balls-Up of Making the Top Four?"

At the moment top four is still in our hands, and if results go a certain way next weekend, we could even have third place in our sights. Now, as up-and-down as this season has been, we would all have given various parts of our body to be in this situation way back in August 2018, wouldn't we?

Still, with our away form as it is, next weekend seems like a long way off, and we have two important games this week. On Thursday

VAR... WHAT IS IT GOOD FOR?

The acronym, VAR, stands for Video Assistant Referee. On the face of it, it's something the game has needed for a very long time. Why is that, though? I think you can probably name a list of reasons, but there is one that is going to come up time and time again; it's because match officials are not very good (that's the polite version, there.)

Why are they not very good? Again, there could be a long list of reasons, most of which would turn the air blue, no doubt.

But, if we were to be really, really, really kind to them, we could say that they are human, and humans make mistakes. (Not gonna lie, I feel dirty being that nice to them.)

For me, the only way VAR can really work, is if it is actually magic. Not just a few people sitting round a screen, not a ref who missed something during a game, but then decides to look at it again on a little telly, only to still give the wrong fucking decision anyway.

No, it has to be actual magic. I don't know how that would work, exactly, I'm not really an expert on magic and stuff, but I've got a box-set of Merlin DVDs laying around somewhere, so I might get back to you on that one.

For now, though, I think I'll reflect on just how completely incompetent and downright useless referees, assistant referees (or linesmen, as we used to know them), third officials and those little blokes that stand behind the goal in European games have been over the years.

It's interesting when you consider how the course of history could have been changed had VAR been available since the beginning of time. "That's impossible" I hear you say, "the technology hasn't been available since the beginning of time..." I hear you add.

Well, maybe the technology hasn't but, as I said, this will only work with the use of magic, and magic has been around for ages.

Time to have a look at a few decisions that, had they been under the spell of VAR, could have changed the world of football as we know it....

(Note – for the following scenarios; assume that magic doesn't exist or is at least banned from being used in football in any way, shape or form, like it was in Merlin.)

Geoff Hurst's World Cup Final Goal

This is the one that immediately springs to mind. Even to this day, there is some doubt as to whether the ball crossed the line and the goal was given correctly.

If that's the case now, could VAR or goal-line technology have proved beyond doubt that it had crossed the line?

You would have to think not, so one of the biggest ever decisions involving England would have been in the hands of someone looking at a screen at the same thing we have for the last 50+ years.

So, there is every chance one of the following could have happened:

1 – 53 years later, and a decision has yet to be made. Players have aged, and some have tragically passed away on the Wembley pitch whilst awaiting the outcome.

2 – the goal is given, and none of our lives have changed.

3 – the goal is not given. Germany go onto win the World Cup, and West Ham fans have fuck all to talk about for 53 years.

Maradona and the "Hand of God"

Another obvious one, especially for England fans. This one is a no-brainer and would surely have resulted in the goal being disallowed.

There's no telling what would've happened after that (although England would probably still have lost.)

One other thing to consider though; could Maradona have been sent off? Maybe not, and maybe he would have received a yellow card, but let's assume that this blatant and disgraceful act of cheating had been punished as severely as we would all loved it to have. His second goal of the game – one that is known as one of the best goals in World Cup history (but is actually one of the world's best players running past players including Steve Hodge and Terry Fenwick), would never have happened.

Mind you, this could all have been avoided in the first place if Peter Shilton hadn't somehow been outjumped by a fucking dwarf.

As an Arsenal supporter, there are many incidents that spring to mind over the years that, had VAR been available, would have been called into question...

The Henchoz Handball Final, 2001

michael owen
@themichaelowen

Just ran over a rabbit.
Devastated.

05/10/2013 19:22

3,514 RETWEETS 1,514 FAVORITES

I'm still pissed off about this game as a whole, to be honest. The Stephane Henchoz handball incident, where he prevented Thierry Henry putting us ahead by handling the ball on the line, was the icing on the cake. A cake made out of poo. A poo cake.

We totally dominated this game. Had VAR been around, then Henchoz would most certainly have been sent off, and Arsenal would have been given a penalty.

Such was our domination when they had eleven men on the pitch, it's hard to imagine anything other than an Arsenal win.

Instead we had to endure that little shit Michael Owen nicking it with two late goals. Owen went on to run over a rabbit with his car years later – an incident which left him "devastated." Who's to say that had the outcome of this game been different, then Owen might not have been driving where he was that fateful night, and that poor little bunny may have still been alive?

Let's hope that VAR is utilised well enough in future to prevent any more rabbit death.

"The 50th Game"

Another game that I'm still pissed off about, and one that a lot of Arsenal fans I know haven't gotten over yet. At a push, I would go as far as to say that Arsenal Football Club still haven't gotten over this game. Something seemed to change in our mentality after this game, and I'm still not convinced we have gotten back whatever we lost on that day, even after many changes in personnel, both at player level, and subsequently at managerial level. Anyway, I'll come back to that, let's discuss "the 50th game" first....

I'm sure most of you know what happened during this game, but for those of you that have been living on the moon, I will try and sum it up as briefly as possible because, in all honesty, if we were to sit here going over every contentious issue in this game, we would be here a long time. Plus, this game still annoys me to the point that I can't actually bring myself to analyse it too much.

Here goes, then...

Arsenal were on 49 games unbeaten, and went to Old Trafford hoping to extend that to a landmark 50 games. Mike Riley then proceeded to give one of the most ridiculously inept display of refereeing you will ever see.

United could have had at least four players sent off, the Neville Brothers kicked the absolute shit out of Jose Antonio Reyes, the penalty for their first goal was a blatant dive from Rooney, Cesc threw pizza at Fergie, the unbeaten run ended on an annoying uneven number, and so goes the song.....

There are many conspiracy theories surrounding this game, and you have to say that's unsurprising. Now, I'm not saying that this display of officiating was bent in any way, but if there was ever a bent display of officiating, you could be forgiven for thinking this display of officiating was bent.

So, would VAR have made a difference? If you haven't seen the game, take a look for yourself. (And by that I mean yes, yes it would....)

"Aguer.... Noooooooooooooooooo"

Life has a funny habit of throwing you a curveball every now and then, doesn't it? Just as I was about to submit this chapter to my good friends at Legends Publishing, and after spending the last few days pondering over examples of why the Virtual Assistant Referee could be a good thing, the Virtual Assistant Referee yanks down his strides and shits all over my chips. The Virtual Arsehole Referee shat on my chips twice tonight, in fact.

Firstly, he (or she, or it, not sure how we're supposed to refer to it... or him... or her. It's probably a "they", but I like to think of it as some kind of entity, rather than a room full of nerds watching the game in slow-motion or something) got my hopes up, when calling the referee to review whether the ball came off of Llorente's arm for the goal which put that lot back in control of their Champions League quarter-final with City. The ref stood at the side of the pitch, looking at it from all angles - at one point I'm sure he was actually almost standing on his head – before deciding it wasn't handball and awarding the goal. No problem with that, to be honest. "Rivalry aside", I actually think it did touch his arm, but at the end of the day, it was in no way definitive. Therein, my friends, lies the problem.

I say the ref decided it wasn't handball, but I'm not sure that was literally the case. I thought, when watching it, that the ref kind of shrugged his shoulders as if to say "mate, I'm not really sure, tbqhwy..." rather than be like, "mate, LOL, that wasn't handball you know...", and so gave the goal.

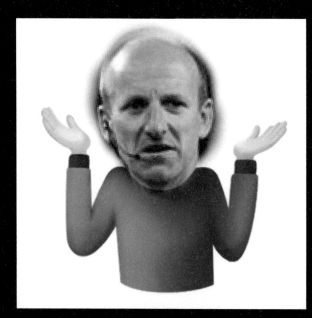

In fact, the "pundits" were still at odds over it after the event, and after the game. I say "at odds" ... Rio Ferdinand thought it was handball, Glen Hoddle, Gary Lineker and, earlier, Jermaine Jenas were adamant that it wasn't handball ... (*rolling eyes emoji*)

That's the point; if a decision is still open to interpretation, and the referee still makes that decision, then what the fuck is the point?

This is where magic needs to come in, isn't it? (Or, we only use technology for situations that can't be open to interpretation, but that would be way too sensible wouldn't it? I think there is probably more chance of using magic than there is using common sense.)

Also, what is the point in leaving the fans on tenterhooks every time a goal is scored? That's the kind of thing that can kill the fans enjoyment of the game, and that is the problem with technology these days isn't it? It's amazing and shit at the same time.

Technology is the reason that we can communicate with people on the other side of the world in a split second, but technology is also the reason that your kids don't talk to you any more (oh, and don't forget the Ian Botham's willy thing that we spoke of earlier on in this journey!)

So, to sum up then; VAR – a good thing or a bad thing? The answer, as is the answer to many a question regarding modern football, not to mention modern life... fuck knows!

we will see whether we will indeed rue those missed chances from the first leg as we take a two-goal lead to Napoli in the quarter final second leg.

Before that though, another huge away game at, erm, Watford. Don't laugh; they're all huge games at the business end.

Monday April 15th, 2019
Watford 0 Arsenal 1

Two and a half minutes into the allotted three minutes of injury time, the Arsenal fans cheered when Bernd Leno kept the ball from going out for a corner. Against ten-man Watford. That pretty much sums up both tonight's performance, and the importance of bagging three points from this game.

Ironically, as we were speaking of tools earlier, Troy Deeney continues to embarrass himself, as his performances against us since his muggy little "cojones" speech, go steadily and hilariously downhill.

At this rate, next time we play them he'll wee his pants, and everyone will point and laugh at him as he has to leave the pitch and put on some pants and shorts from lost property. He will then be known as "pissy pants Troy" for the rest of his life.

His latest moment of hilarity came after a mad few minutes early on in the game. On ten minutes, Aubameyang closed down a day-dreaming Ben Foster, and the keeper's attempted clearance ricocheted off of Auba's leg and into the net. Moments later, pissy pants Troy was sent for an early bath, after catching Torreira with this arm.

He knew what he was doing; it was a deliberate act, from an arrogant, stupid player. It was a nailed-on straight red.

Troy Deeney knows that. We all know that. How do we know?

BECAUSE THE SILLY MAN TOLD US OVER A YEAR AGO WHAT HE WAS GOING TO DO!

"I have to watch what I say, but it's (having) a bit of cojones, is what I'll say. Whenever I play against Arsenal, I'll go up and think 'let me whack the first one and see who wants it."

Doesn't really make sense anyway, does it?

"I have to watch what I say, but I'll say it anyway..."

Arsehole.

As far as I'm concerned, this is just another in a long line of extremely average footballers using The Arsenal as an attention-seeking exercise. In fact, the thing that annoyed me about that "cojones" nonsense was the fact that so many Arsenal fans openly agreed with him. Maybe he did have a point, but that's, erm, not the point. Still, each to their own and all that.

The rest of the game is as memorable as it needs to be, in the way that it's best forgotten. It doesn't matter how you win at the business end of the season, the only thing that matters is that you do win. There is a lot to be said for winning ugly at the business end of the season and, man, this wasn't just ugly; this was Troy Deeney ugly. The mood of the Arsenal fans after the game reflected all of the above. Come to think of it, the mood of the Arsenal fans during the game reflected all of the above.

It's not as if the clickbait hounds would let us forget the game easily though, is it? Oh no. This week it was the turn of the almost perfectly named Jason Cundy - Ex-Tottenham and Chelsea "star", now "star" of pathetic wind-up radio station TalkSport.

I can't really be bothered to go into it in too much detail, but he basically went down the tried and tested "bait the Arsenal fans" route frequented by ex-footballers that don't have a proper job and insisted that Deeney shouldn't have been sent off, more or less blamed Torriera for being the right height for his head to connect with Deeney's arm, he made a meal of it, football is a contact sport... etc, etc, etc... Textbook stuff. Some people still bite at this stuff, I myself prefer to mock.

With that in mind, I tried looking up Cundy's career achievements, and it reads even worse than Danny Rose's did when I looked him up a couple of months back.

Indeed, Rose's Sunderland Young Player of the Season 2012-13 may as well be a Ballon d'or compared to Cundy's most memorable career moment. This is from his Wikipedia page....

"Cundy is remembered for the "freak" goal that he scored against Ipswich Town in a Premiership match for Tottenham, in 1992–93. In an attempt to kick the ball 40 yards from goal, he slipped and managed a wind-assisted effort that ended up flying over 'keeper Craig Forrest and into the back of the net. The goal was captured live on Sky Sports and put Spurs 1–0 up, in a match that finished 1–1."

Wow. Lionel Messi eat your heart out eh?

Other than that, the only other thing of note about Jason Cundy is that his face looks like it's been put on the wrong head. Anyway, moving on.

Thursday April 18th, 2019
Napoli 0 Arsenal 1

As I've not seen much of this game, I'm going to keep this short and sweet. I was intending to watch it, but I decided to join my wife and kids down in Clacton where they had been for the week. The lure of ridiculously low-priced beer, fish and chips and sea air was a lot greater than sitting at home watching the game in my boxers with a few cans, to be honest. I tried a battered Mars bar as well (it was surprisingly good!)

As far as the game went; the classic One-Nil to The Arsenal away from home in Europe was exactly what the doctor ordered.

A superb free-kick from Laca on 36 minutes gave us the away goal, and left the hosts needing four to beat us. They were never coming back from this. Job well and truly done, and we go into the semi-finals against Valencia.

A European semi-final. I will certainly settle for that right now. Obviously, there is a very real chance my mindset will completely change in the next few days... but, as I've said time and time again; such is the rollercoaster world of the Arsenal supporter!

Week 36
April 21st - 27th, 2019
Losers Weepers

After all the ups and downs this season, today we find ourselves with a third-place finish in the Premier League in our hands.

It's quite amazing really and is, to be brutally honest as much to do with the form of the teams that are battling it out for the top four with us.

It's also amazing because, the team currently sitting in third position have lost more games than us.

Even more amazing is the fact that the team currently sitting in third position are football's latest superpower. Perhaps that is their actual superpower; is it a bird, is it a plane.... no... it's SUPERSPURS! The club with the superhuman ability to sit third in the Premier League table having lost more games than the team in fifth!

To be even more brutally honest, though, who gives a shit why or how we finish in the top four? I don't.

If you care about that sort of thing, then you are probably the kind of person that, if you saw someone walk away from a cash-point having forgot to take their money with them, you would run after them to give it to them. I'm not that guy. Finder's keepers.

The only thing we should be giving a shit about, at the business end of the season is IF we finish in the top four.

Having said all of this, I am, of course, far from confident that we will take advantage of this opportunity that has been presented to us. We do have a home game to kick off the week, though, so who knows. Anyway, I'm off to sunny Southend for a few beers in the sun today, so I will no doubt experience the joy that is following an Arsenal match on Twitter this afternoon. Can. Not. Wait!

Sunday April 21st, 2019
Arsenal 2 Crystal Palace 3

So, Arsenal fans, how do you fancy having a go at solving a simple maths problem? Of course you do. Okay, here goes....

If you had a pound for every time that the words "...in our hands" were mentioned before a game, and we proceeded to make a spectacular balls up of it, meaning that the words "...no longer in our hands" were mentioned after the game, how many pounds would you have?

Answer; a lot of pounds.

What is there to say about this game?

Before this game, we had third place in our hands. Win, and we move above SuperSpurs.

We lost 3-2 at home to Crystal Palace.

Emery played around with the starting line-up, including starts for Gooner Jenko, Elneny and Mavropanos.

The formation was completely the wrong formation.

Mustafi did a big Mustafi.

That will do I think.

The end.

Surely, with just a few games left, we should be picking the best team available for every game, no?

Still, at least our away form is superb, and we don't have a tricky game at Wolves coming up next, eh? Oh.....

Wednesday April 24th, 2019
Wolves 3 Arsenal 1

Remember a few weeks back when I said I'm going to form my opinion on the manager game-by-game? Well, this week's take is a huge poo emoji.

As I've said already; on Saturday afternoon, after Spurs had lost to Man City, we had Champions League qualification in our hands. In fact, we actually had third place back in our hands.

On Sunday, while United were doing their bit by being turned over by Everton, we proceeded to lose at home to Palace.

Chelsea then did their bit on Monday night, being held to a 2-2 draw at home to Burnley.

I also said a few weeks back, that I can see us losing every one of our remaining away games. We managed to scrape a win at Watford by winning Troy Deeney ugly, and I began to think that maybe, just maybe, we could drag ourselves over the line, make the top four, then sort ourselves out over the summer.

This is the story of my Arsenal life over the last few years, and why I've struggled to find the energy for it all.

Just as I think I'm out, they pull me back in again.

Then, just as they're pulling me back in, they shit me right back out again.

They shit me out on Sunday, and tonight they pulled the chain. The thing is, a 45-year old turd such as me is almost impossible to flush.

(I really must apologise for the crudeness of that analogy and any visuals you may have formed with it, but you have to admit it kind of hits the nail on the head doesn't it?)

3-0 down at half-time. Game over.

We got a late consolation from Sokratis, but that's hardly worth mentioning. Late consolations are never worth mentioning. That's why they're called late consolations. If they were worth mentioning, they would be called "late things worth mentioning", but they are not.

Unsurprisingly, there was much unrest amongst the Arsenal online fanbase in the following days, with the nagging doubts that some had surrounding the manager growing into something more than nagging. What's worse than nagging? I'm going to say poking.

Yes, poking.

When the doubts were just standing there nagging at us, annoying as they were, it was easier to ignore them than it was before they started poking us.

If we had won at least one of the last two games, the doubts might have just stood there and carried on nagging, and just gently tapping us every now and then. But no, here they are poking away like, erm, pokey things.

They don't seem to nag, tap or poke everyone though.

There are those that were nagged, tapped, poked, kicked, punched, stamped on and battered across the face with a brick by doubt during the latter years of Arsene Wenger's reign, that they refused to be nagged any more. There are also the ultra-positive types that have never been nagged in their lives, such is their ultra-positivity.

Anyway, I digress. To sum this week up in a nutshell; at this moment in time. I really do not like football.

We have another away game at the weekend, at Leicester. Time to take a break until then, and consign the last couple of games to the scrapheap that is made up of various disappointments served up by the football team I support over the years.

Week 37
April 28th – May 5th, 2019
The Race for Not Top Four

"Welcome to Sky Sports Super Sunday. Today we turn our attention to the race to finish outside of the top four, which is really hotting up, with Tottenham, Arsenal, Chelsea and Manchester United doing their best to out-shit each other every week.

Arsenal, who find themselves in the driving seat for a not top four finish after conceding six goals in two games, face Leicester today at the King Power and, considering their away form for the last two years, they'll be looking to further cement a position that, just a few weeks ago seemed highly unlikely…"

Sunday April 28th, 2019
Leicester City 3 Arsenal 0

I've decided that I am now done with holding my head up high and doing my best to be proud of everything The Arsenal stands for as a club. I'm fed up with being patient and having faith that one day we will succeed in doing things "the right way." The good guys don't win any more, this ain't fucking Star Wars, mate. It was fun (no it wasn't, really) giving it a go but, as the saying goes; Enough is Enough; It's Time for Change. "History, tradition and class"? You can shove it, mate. As for "self-sustainability", if I want to hear about that, I'll watch The Good Life on UK Gold.

Yes, I have decided that I want Arsenal to become one of those Sugar Daddy clubs. I can't ever remember Chelsea and Manchester City really being very good before the dodgy dough turned up. It's that simple. Get a rich bloke to buy the club and throw billions of pounds at it, then you win things. Okay, it might get a bit boring, but it's getting boring watching Man City winning everything to be quite honest.

It doesn't have to be boring, though. Not if we do it all bigger and better than anyone else. I want an owner *so* rich that we can do literally anything we want. I want us to buy Messi and Ronaldo. I want us to buy Messi, Ronaldo and Neymar. I want us to buy players just so nobody else can have them (like Chelsea and Mourinho used to.)

I want an owner *so* rich that he shits gold and wipes his bum with his servants' faces.

I'm not worried about what that might mean to the future of the club, because I don't want the club to have a future. I want us to spend so much money that we are talking self-destruction rather than self-sufficiency.

It will have been worth it. Watching the club self-destruct couldn't be any more painful than watching us concede nine goals against Crystal Palace, Wolves and Leicester in the space of one poxy week.

So, who is this person that would be willing to ride in on his red and white horse and save us? I don't particularly care, as long as he has a massive pile of cash and no moral compass. Anyway... the game.

Once again, we were on the wrong end of some shocking officiating, as young Maitland-Niles was sent off for two yellow cards, the first of which was an absolute joke, to be honest.

It was a foul, yes, but never a yellow.

He may have been slightly naïve making the tackle for the second one, but the fact is that he should never have been on a booking in the first place. Also, on closer viewing the second one was made to look worse by the Leicester player, which pretty much sums this refereeing performance up.

In his post-match analysis, Graeme Souness then pretty much summed todays commentary performance up when he got it arse-upwards and decided that the first one was a booking and the second one was harsh.

Sky's commentary really wound me up today. It wound me up more than the football, to be honest, as I'm currently resigned to Arsenal never winning a Premier League match away from home again.

It can be summed up by Alan Smith's (and whatever div was commentating with him, the name escapes me) reaction when Choudhury, whom it was clear from the outset was Sky Sports favourite of the week, fouled Torreira but there wasn't even a free kick given. They then watched the replay, which clearly showed a foul, then continued to praise the lad.

The game was dead after the red card, and I will never speak of it again. In fact, from now until the end of the season, my plan is to not speak about the football if we lose a match. That's it, I'm done with it.

So, from having third place in our hands to pole position in the race for not top four in that space of a couple of weeks. I really just want this season to be finished.

The one saving grace at the moment is, of course, the Europa League. The one thing that can make this season worthwhile. I have to say that, at the moment, I would be fully behind ending the season early if things don't go well in the first leg on Thursday. In fact, had the first leg been away from home, I would have been fully behind ending the season right now. As it is, the first leg is at home, and this feels like the biggest game of the season so far, maybe even the biggest game of the last two seasons. I suppose that is something to be thankful for, as the league campaign stutters to a painful end.

Thursday May 2nd, 2019
Arsenal 3 Valencia 1

This was hanging by a thread right up until the death, due to the prehistoric relic that is the away goals rule. A rule that has kicked us in the balls more times over the years than I can remember. Make no mistake, the difference between 2-1 and 3-1 is absolutely massive. So much so, that when watching it at 2-1, it didn't even feel as though that would be a win! Crazy when you think of it, but that's where we are, and that's how completely stupid the away goals rule is.

Honestly, 2-1 would have felt like a loss right now.

"What was the score tonight then?"

"We lost 2-1"

"Oh shit, that's not good. They've got two away goals."

"No, they've only got one."

"But I thought you said...."

"Look, I'm tired, it's been a long season and I'm not in the mood to explain, so just forget it OKAY?!"

We even went a goal down after eleven minutes.... well of course we did! That feeling of impending doom didn't last long though, as two goals from Laca meant we were 2-1 up just fourteen minutes later.

You would think that would make things more comfortable for us fans, but when all that means is that a 1-0 win for Valencia in the second leg would take them through, then it hardly seemed worth it!

Still, as it stands, Auba's last minute goal to put us 3-1 up, coming at a time when apparently half of the stadium had already gone home, has put us within touching distance of the final. I must say I'm extremely confident now. That's how fine that line is.

Week 38
May 5th – 12th, 2019
Fine Lines

A lot going on this week, the last week of the league season. Two more games and it's done. The line between success and failure, between progress and no progress, is at its finest.

We go into the Europa League semi-final second leg at the Mestalla with a two-goal cushion, with the chance of making the final in the Arse-end of Nowhere Stadium, Baku, Azerbaijan.

As painful as this season has been - especially the last few months – if we were to win a trophy, then surely even the most miserable among us would have to be the slightest bit happy with that. I know I will.

Should we not win it, then I really don't know how I'll feel about this season. I've been massively pissed off with the way things have gone over the last couple of months or so, but I'm desperately clinging to the hope of a European final (ok it's not THE European final, but it is technically a European final), and a good old knees up in Islington should we win it. (There will probably be more people in The Famous Cock at Highbury Corner than there will be in the stadium by the looks of it.) Before that though, we have the chance to cement our position in the battle for not top four with our last home game of the season, against Brighton.

Sunday May 5th, 2019
Arsenal 1 – Brighton 1

I can think of a no more fitting way than to hand you over to the official club website's match report for this one… "Our hopes of securing a top-four place are effectively over after we could only draw with Brighton in our final home match of the season.

Having seen Chelsea win 3-0 before kick-off, we knew that we needed to do the same to keep our hopes alive – and we made the perfect start.

Henrikh Mkhitaryan hit the post with little more than 60 seconds on the clock, and we continued to press and were soon awarded a penalty when Nacho Monreal was bundled over in the area by Alireza Jahanbakhsh. Pierre-Emerick Aubameyang stepped up and made no mistake to give us the early advantage, but in truth we failed to build on it for much of a sluggish first half.

But we came to life just before the interval as Shkodran Mustafi, Aubameyang and Mkhitaryan all tested Mat Ryan into action in quick succession during an intense spell.

But it was Bernd Leno who was busier at the start of the second half, and he had to get down well to make a smart save to deny Solly March. We were soon made to pay for our lack of intensity when March went down in the area under a Granit Xhaka challenge and Glenn Murray converted from the spot. Our top-four hopes were now hanging by a thread – how would we respond?

Back we came, with Aubameyang soon volleying over after meeting a Xhaka corner, before the Gabon international then fired wide from 10 yards out. Brighton came within inches of snatching a late win as Gross sliced a shot wide from close range but try as we might, we could find no way through as a hugely disappointing afternoon came to a close."

Two reasons why I've not done my own report on the match (not that I usually do much of a match report anyway.)

Firstly, I just can't be bothered with it at the moment. As I said last week, I just want the league season to be over and done with now. I will be 100% buzzing for the game on Thursday, it's almost as if it's a completely different ball game. There's that fine line again.

Secondly, I think even the tone of that match report on the official site sounds like it's had enough as well, so they've done that job for me.

Monday morning, and it seems as though I'm not the only one that wants this season to end. We are all clinging on to the fact that we could still end up having a more successful season than that lot up the road, and those other media darlings Liverpool.

"THE INVINCIBLES WERE A MYTH!" ADRIAN DURHAM, TALKSPORT

Adrian Durham is a strange little man, isn't he? Okay, I know that it's his job to outrage people to the point that they actually listen to his crappy little radio show, but that's not exactly an achievement to be proud of is it?

Or maybe it is, I don't know. The fact that he has one of those faces that people want to clobber means he's found his perfect vocation in life. How many people can genuinely say that? It took me half my life!

Plus, even after all this time, and despite anyone with half a brain in their head being fully aware of what he's up to, people STILL BITE! Maybe he's actually a genius. He's not, he's a twat in many peoples' eyes judging by the amount of times that word is posted on his Twitter timeline.

In this particular "rant", he claimed that the Invincibles are a myth because they lost games that season.

"Arsenal's Invincibles lost crucial games that season.

They lost Champions League group stage games to Inter and Kyiv. They lost home and away to Middlesbrough in the semi-finals of the League Cup – they fielded a decent side as well. They lost to

Man United in the FA Cup. Not exactly Invincible, were they then?"

Okay, Adrian, we'll call ourselves the Premier League Invincibles, is that better? Perhaps not...

"Wenger was obsessed with going unbeaten. So obsessed he didn't even try to win games as the season came to an end.

He was happy to draw four of the last six – including home to Birmingham! Anyone saying the so-called Invincibles are the best ever has lost their mind completely.

The Invincibles were a myth!"

The great thing about this is that, during this "rant", he seems more wound up by that squad being known as The Invincibles, than we are about some dickhead ranting about it.

He also "places Jose Mourinho's first Chelsea team of 2004/05 ahead of the Gunners – as they won more points."

A Chelsea team that drew the same amount of games that finished in second place that season.

That team? Yep, you guessed it, The Arsenal.

All boxes have been ticked there – mention that we drew league games, mention that we lost cup games, and a nice juicy bonus for mentioning Chelsea and Mourinho (whilst neglecting to mention the fact that Chelsea side were bankrolled by a multi-billionaire...)

Fluent Clickbait.

Genius or twat? You decide.

I could probably write an entire book of Arsenal clickbait. There are that many examples out there! I've limited the number of examples I am going to use, however, as if I'm honest, it would bore the arse off of me just compiling it, let alone you anyone having to read it.

There were a few that missed out, including the famous Arsenal Bin Bag protest that never happened, and the Daily Mirror listing "11 Things Stronger than Jack Wilshere's Ankles", after Jack was sidelined for three months due to another ankle operation. This came complete with "Share your suggestions on Twitter" at the end of it, and raised two questions for me: 1 – why 11? 2 – how is a highly talented young English player undergoing a major operation funny? You wankers.

As I say, the list is almost endless. You know what, though? I think the best thing is to continue to react to these people. Give them the attention they crave, but don't bite... they like it when you bite. It's almost a fetish for them, and the thought of Adrian Durham and Jason Cundy sitting there rubbing each other because they've hooked you is enough to scar anyone for life.

Don't' bite, just mock them. Mock them and laugh at them. Job done.

Despite us beating our North London neighbours in the battle for not top four, we could still end up with more silverware than them, as they are an away goal down in their Champions League semi-final with Ajax, whom they face in the second leg tomorrow.

As for the "Scouse, not English" mob, they are 3-0 down from the first leg with Barcelona, and with the league in City's hands, are on the verge of winning sod all, despite the season-long collective media bukkake over them. If those two games go to plan, and ours does too, then I might just like football again. Fast forward to Thursday morning.

By now, you'll know exactly what happened in the other two games, so let's not speak of them ever again. The Bad Thing has happened, and at this particular moment in time, I couldn't hate football more.

To have to want Liverpool to win the Champions League (as any self-respecting Arsenal supporter should), is something I can't even begin to contemplate at the moment. There is of course a much worse scenario that could play out, and that is one that I can't even contemplate contemplating.

It's all on the lads tonight to make me like football again, the finest of fine lines is so fine at the moment, it's barely even a line. To paraphrase Joey Tribbiani; the line is a dot to me.

It's time to forget the Champions League exists for a few hours, and hope that two dramatic comebacks are all that those cruel footballing gods will bestow upon us for one week.

ATTENTION PLEASE

**WE INTERRUPT THIS SEASON TO BRING
YOU BREAKING NEWS**

**A STATE OF EMERGENCY HAS BEEN DECLARED IN NORTH
LONDON, AFTER TOTTENHAM HOTSPUR TONIGHT REACHED
THE FINAL OF THE CHAMPIONS LEAGUE.
PLEASE READ ON FOR IMPORTANT INSTRUCTIONS ON WHAT
TO DO SHOULD THE UNTHINKABLE HAPPEN.**

The Champions League final takes place in Madrid on Saturday June 2nd, the following guidelines are designed for your safety should the match be won by Tottenham Hotspur.

DELETE THE INTERNET

Naturally; all social media must go. But you are advised to also destroy any device that may expose you to fallout. This includes mobile phones, computers, televisions, radios (do people still have those?) and those Alexa things.

BOOK THE DAY OFF OF WORK IN ADVANCE

This won't matter too much in the long run anyway because, if you have any sense, you are going to a place far away from here. You are, however, advised to book Monday June 4th off of work NOW. This will ensure that your evacuation goes without a hitch. You DO NOT want your evacuation to be delayed due to being arrested for murder (if you're fortunate enough to not work with Tottenham fans, there's always one c**t that all of a sudden becomes a football fan after a result like this isn't there? Or "Isn't it great that the London team won?" No, Malcolm, it is not.)

BE PREPARED

Travel as lightly as possible, and pack only the essentials. The evacuation will have to be quick, and you must be prepared to leave as soon as you hear the final whistle.

You are, however, advised to pack as much alcohol, and as many drugs that you can get your hands on.

THE EVACUATION

Don't even wait for the final whistle if it looks like they're going to win it. Get yourself out the front door as quickly as possible and make your escape.

BUT WHERE DO YOU GO?

After having done extensive research, it can be confirmed that the most suitable place for evacuees is on the planet Tatooine. This is where Ben "Obi Wan" Kenobi fled to after the fall of the Jedi Order, moving into an abandoned moisture prospectors' home in the Jundland Wastes, situated on a bluff surrounded by the Western Dune Sea. He lived there untroubled as a kind of hermit for 19 years. (Until Luke Skywalker rocked up, but that's a whole other story.)

**DO NOT, UNDER ANY CIRCUMSTANCES TRY TO "FRONT IT."
THIS WILL NOT END WELL. YOU MUST, I REPEAT MUST,
LEAVE THE PLANET.**

Stay safe, my fellow Arsenal fans.

Thursday May 9th, 2019
Valencia 2 Arsenal 4

I challenge you to find an Arsenal fan alive that didn't fear the worst when Kevin Gameiro gave Valencia the lead after just eleven minutes. The collapse was coming, we could feel it. It didn't come. Amongst all the frustration and general misery, there is one thing that has shone brighter than anything else this season, and that is Lacabameyang. Not just the goals, but these are two players that love playing together. It's the kind of partnership that deserves a trophy. I don't mean that in a literal sense, of course. I'm not a scouser.

Auba had a stormer, his best game in an Arsenal shirt. The expected collapse was only a worry for six minutes, as he fired in an absolute peach from 20 yards, after being set up by Laca, and our two-goal cushion was restored. On fifty minutes, the pair combined again, this time Laca was the goalscorer. This meant Valencia needed to score four, and even this Arsenal were not going to let that happen. Auba went on to score a hat-trick, and we are in a European final. The only European final that is happening this year, as the season now ends on May 29th, 2019. Anything that happens after that is nothing more than a figment of someone else's imagination. After a few weeks of treading that fine line, I like football again tonight.

I must admit I had forgotten that we still have one more league game to play, and there is still an outside chance of failure in the battle for not top four. All it needs for that to happen is an eight-goal turnaround with the team above us. Stranger, or should I say similar, things have actually happened.

Sunday May 12th, 2019
Burnley 1 Arsenal 3

So, that's it. The end of the Premier League season. Results around us meant that we secured our place in the battle for not top four, finishing fifth, a point behind the New Footballing Superpower.

A brace for Auba means that he shares the golden boot with Salah and Mane. I'm not quite sure how that works, if he gets it every third weekend or something, but it shows how important a player he's been for us this season. It was nice to see young Eddie Nketiah score his first Premier League goal as well, as he sealed the result in injury time.

Not really much to say about this season that hasn't already been said from an Arsenal point of view, to be honest.

Elsewhere, it was truly heart-warming to see plucky little Manchester City win the Premier League. It's been a real Cinderella story this season, watching them brush aside all-comers, despite only having a bottomless pit of cash to spend. Pep Guardiola once again proved what a fantastic coach he is, having only previously coached at clubs with billions of pounds to spend. Bless him.

Runners-up were Liverpool, who hilariously managed to lose just one game all season – less than City – and still not win the league.

That, my friends, is that. Of course, we have the small matter of the Europa League final in just over a fortnight, which also means that I have another couple of weeks to finish writing this book!

Weeks 39 & 40
The Post Premier League Lull

Thanks to our participation in the Europa League Final, our season will now end a couple of weeks later than the Premier League season. There are other issues to deal with before that, though. We wouldn't just give ourselves a break and recharge our batteries, would we?

Firstly, there is the customary summer tradition that is transfer speculation, which begins before the last ball of the season has even been kicked.

This basically consists (as is the case with every transfer window) of some obscure "football" websites or Twitter accounts throwing a number of names out into the virtual crowd, followed by weeks of speculation by grown adults that really should have better things to do. We spoke about the dreaded "ITK", back in January.

January is nothing more than a warmup for the real thing for them, however, and these creatures are to be avoided at all costs during the summer. If we were praying for the end of the season just a few weeks ago, then exposure to these vile beings will have you praying for the end of the summer in no time. That is not a good thing. Summer is good.

There are also grown adults who will create their own lists of players that they think Arsenal should buy. This often leads to discussions on Twitter that last for days, and in the end, everyone has forgotten that the whole discussion began in the mind of some geezer off of Twitter. Even the geezer himself has forgotten that. Then you have people witnessing the tail-end of the discussion, who aren't even aware that it began in the mind of some Twitter geezer, and take it as read that Arsenal have actually been linked with said player or players.

There is also the question of the budget available. Someone touts a figure, and the moment this figure is announced, it just seems to stick.

If you scrolled really quickly through your timeline a few weeks ago and closed your eyes straight after, all you would see was "£40m." Once it's burned into your retina, it's burned into your brain, and all transfer speculation revolves around that figure, including from people that apparently know that the £40m figure isn't accurate!

The bottom line is this; I don't know how much money Arsenal have to spend during the summer, and I have no idea who they will spend it on. Neither do you, so shut up and go outside, you weirdo. The trend of creating lists doesn't end there, though.

Before the league season had even ended, people began listing the current squad, and telling us which players should be kept on, and which ones should be binned. A green tick for keeping, a red "X" for binning.

If we're lucky, we may even get the odd question mark (the question mark will usually be attributed to a player that it's not obvious

HAPPY INVINCIBLES DAY!

May 15th, 2004. The day that history was made, as Arsenal beat Leicester 2-1 at Highbury, meaning we had gone a whole league season unbeaten.

I was at the game, and I said to myself, admittedly with a lump in my throat, that this would never be done again. Maybe it will, but I've been right so far.

As far as I'm concerned, this was the best squad the Premier League has seen. Yes, I am biased, but they were a genuine phenomenon. A squad of players hitting their collective peak, a team that would win games before a ball had even been kicked.

A general theme throughout this book has been the way that the media loves to bait Arsenal fans, and there is no greater bait than belittling the Invincibles.

Let them belittle us. The more they do it, the better it feels.

Whatever they say, the invincible season is something that every Arsenal supporter should be proud of until the end of time. Legendary.

As I mentioned earlier, every season, whenever a team have gone a few games unbeaten, they are touted as "the next Invincibles."

Cue the Arsenal online fanbase jumping in, in their thousands, to defend what was, in my opinion, the greatest team the Premier League has ever seen.

The thing with this is, that as much as the media do this to wind Arsenal fans up, the truth of the matter (in my opinion anyway), is the fact that The Arsenal went a whole season without being beaten in the league winds people up more than they could possibly wind us up.

"They drew too many games…"

"They lost cup games and Champions League games; how can they be Invincible…?"

We shrug our shoulders and grin the smuggest of grins. The type of grin that you can only bear when you know you have gotten under somebody's skin.

City win the league with 100 points - "is this a greater achievement than Arsenal's Invincibles?" they ask.

"Ours is gold", we answer. And there it is.

There are no ifs and buts as far as that goes; The Arsenal went a League season without losing a single game, and that is fact. Anything else is nothing but opinion.

Some people have the opinion that the Earth is flat.

There are people that watch Big Brother, The Only Way is Essex, Love Island and all that other "reality" nonsense, and believe it's real and not 100% fake, staged horseshit, Clickbait TV! Enough said.

I've already covered what was, for me, probably the worst example of Clickbait ever, in Adrian Durham's "The Invincibles Were a Myth!" tripe.

Adrian Durham. A man that appears to spend most of his life spouting nonsense, with the sole purpose of winding people up and getting a reaction. That may be his job, but I couldn't care less. Get a proper job, you pillock.

Imagine that being your job. Imagine that being your life.

Imagine having to look your family in the eye when you sit round the dinner table of an evening, and they ask you how your day was.

"It was great! I argued with angry men on the phone and blocked over 500 people on Twitter for calling me a nonce!"

I am aware that it's not only Arsenal fans that are targeted, but there was once a section of Durham's show called "The Daily Arsenal." Pathetic.

Apologies for the slight digression there, but let's be honest, when has there ever been a wrong time to remind ourselves of what a grade A donut Durham is? Anyway… Happy Invincibles Day!

whether it's the "in" thing to either keep or bin; nobody wants to make themselves look daft with this particular form of attention seeking.) It's like some twisted version of "Snog Marry Avoid."... "Keep Bin Not Sure Because I Don't Know What People Will Say", perhaps.

There is an extension to this game too, where players are given ratings for the season. These should be avoided at all costs unless, of course, you have an inclination to give some berk a few quid by clicking through to their YouTube channel.

Having said that, there are people out there who do this sort of thing because they have a genuine passion for talking about football, rather than a genuine passion for ad revenue and attention, so seek those out instead. If you can't tell the difference by now, then you deserve all you get.

Thankfully, a few things that actually matter have cropped up to occupy those of us that have more of an interest in football than impressing strangers on the internet or dicking about in front of a camera, as the Europa League descends into a complete farce.

As if getting to Baku wasn't hard enough for the fans, it has been announced that Henrikh Mkhitaryan has decided not to travel to the final at all, because of concerns over his safety due to his country's conflict with Azerbaijan. This situation is just ridiculous beyond words.

Miki may not have started the game, he may not be everyone's cup of tea, but at the end of the day, we have been deprived of an experienced player. A player that has won the Europa League before, actually scoring in the final (and he's scored against Chelsea), due to reasons that have nothing whatsoever to do with football. Un-bloody-believable.

I'm sure someone somewhere is bathing in cash due to the decision to hold the final in Baku, and I'm sure these people could not give a flying fuck about football supporters anywhere.

I've spoken a number of times about my fading love for the game; this is the kind of thing that will see that love continue to fade.

There is talk of boycotting the game, of making a stand, but for me the best way to make a stand is to win the thing, then shove it right back up their arse.

There is talk that Petr Cech will take up a position with Chelsea next season, leading to suggestions that, due to this, he shouldn't start the final. I say suggestions; in some places it's complete and utter outrage.

There is a case that Leno should start because he's currently the better keeper, but any suggestion that Cech will be anything other than professional are complete nonsense.

I have a feeling that the farce that is the Europa League final will see a few more ridiculous turns over the next week, but in truth it's all just a way of passing time in the lead up to the final. The season has gone on for far too long, let's just get the bastard thing over and done with, PLEASE!

Europa or Bust

Looking back to the beginning of this book, the beginning of the season, our expectations were low in regard to what we might achieve. Most of us were happy to give the manager a free pass for his first season in charge, because this wasn't about immediate success, this was about moving forward.

Moving forward wasn't about winning trophies immediately, it was about starting afresh. The beginning of a new era. An end to the never-ending cycle of monotony that supporting The Arsenal had become. This was New Arsenal.

The thing is, all of that goes against the grain when it comes to supporting a football club.

It's a stance that is nigh on impossible to maintain throughout the rollercoaster ride that is the football season.

It's incredibly difficult to acknowledge, back in August that, come May, you'll have nothing to celebrate other than coming through a season filled with cautious optimism for the next one. This season has been the perfect example of that rollercoaster ride.

It's only natural that expectations are raised when you go on a 22-game unbeaten run. You begin to think "what if?"

It's only natural that expectations are raised when you have a third placed finish in your own hands with just a few weeks of the season remaining.

It's only natural, then, when your expectations are raised to that point, you've completely forgotten how low they were in the first place.

Having little to no expectations at the beginning of the season is also a weird feeling when you come to judge the season in terms of success, progress or failure. I could be here all week discussing the permutations and implications, so the best I can do is this:

Win the Europa League, and we've had a successful season.

Silverware = success.

I'm old-fashioned in that respect.

Lose the final, and I'm going to have to look back on the season as a disappointment.

Okay, expectations were low back in August, but lose this game and, for me personally, they will be even lower this August. Unless, of course, we have an incredible summer of transfer activity but... well... I'm sure I wouldn't be the only one to be staggered should that happen. Harsh, maybe, but that's where I'm at right now.

As well as that; try as I might, it's impossible to forget the other European final that takes place this week, the possible outcome of which is genuinely terrifying. The possible outcomes are as follows:

Arsenal lose, Tottenham lose.

We will be massively disappointed but can seek solace in the fact that after all is said and done, the bottom line is that their season has been better than ours by a single point.

Arsenal win, Tottenham lose.

We are back in the Champions League, we've won a trophy and they haven't. This is the best possible outcome this week, unless someone invents a way in which Tottenham and Liverpool can both lose the same game.

Arsenal win, Tottenham win.

As delighted as we will all be on Wednesday night should we bring home the Europa League, there is every chance that it could all come crashing down should this happen. We'll have to hear about how we've won the budget European trophy while they've won the real thing, and we will have to hear about that until the end of time.

Arsenal lose, Tottenham win.

End of days stuff. I'm finding it difficult to put this into words, as I don't think I can even contemplate it happening. The worst possible outcome, and one that will take a long time to go away. I'm going to leave it at that, as it's a genuinely sickening thought.

In conclusion, the best thing that can happen this week is an Arsenal win and a Spurs loss. Literally nothing good can come from that lot winning the big one. Nothing.

Even losing to Chelsea in the final, and Ferry Cross the Fucking Mersey being piped into every home in the country for the next 300 years couldn't be as painful as that.

Right, it's the day before the game, and time to put all thoughts of The Bad Thing to one side, it's all about The Arsenal for now.

Bricking It

So, after initially deciding to leave the writing alone and try and take my mind off the game until kick off, here I am writing about it. With clenched buttocks. Apologies for that particular image, but I doubt there's an Arsenal fan alive that doesn't know exactly what I mean. If there is, then I want some of the drugs you're on, please.

For a fanbase that has been so notoriously fractured in recent times, there is nothing like a cup final to unite us, and we are not only united in our support for The Arsenal in one of the biggest games we've faced in recent years. No; we are united because we are all crapping ourselves. Social media can be great on days like this, but by late afternoon... not so much.

It's all well and good spending all morning discussing among ourselves how impossible we are finding it to concentrate, with a bit of gallows humour thrown in. The problem is that the later it gets the worse you realise that's made you feel. By which time it's too sodding late!

So, here I am on the train home, at 16.53, waffling away like an idiot to you all, in an attempt to take my mind off of the game.

It hasn't worked, and now I feel sick.

We really don't help ourselves, do we?

To Hell and Baku
The Europa League Final
Wednesday May 26th, 2019
Chelsea 4 Arsenal 1
NO NO NO NO NO NO NOOOOOOO!!! Giroud...

It just had to be him didn't it? Chelsea may have gone on to score three more goals but, make no mistake, this Arsenal team were beaten the moment Olivier Giroud put them ahead on 49 minutes.

I thought the heads went down noticeably, straight away.

Olivier Giroud won the Europa League for Chelsea.

Talk like that would have had you carted off by the men in white coats not so long ago.

We started decently enough, looked sharper than Chelsea, and we could have had a penalty (it would have been harsh, in my opinion, but as the saying goes; we've seen them given), but once Chelsea had created a couple of decent chances, the feeling of having seen this movie before, and it never ends well, inevitably crept in. The collapse was coming, we all knew it, and boy... did we collapse.

If we're honest, this was the culmination of a couple of months or so of dreadful form, with the semi-final against Valencia being the exception rather than the rule. Embarrassing.

With 63 minutes gone we were.... actually, fuck this.

You all know how crap we were; you all know how bleak the future is looking, and what a monumental task we have in front of us to get anywhere near where The Arsenal should be, and the challenges ahead of us to get there.

I've not spent the last nine months of my life on my first book for it to end like this. No way, mate.

Ever seen Wayne's World?

Let's do the Scooby Doo ending...

The Scooby Doo Ending

Wow. To say we didn't see that coming is quite the understatement! I mean, how could anyone?! The football world is in a state of shock today, after the Europa League final descended into chaos during what was supposed to be the presentation of the trophy to Chelsea, after they defeated Arsenal 4-1.

As Petr Cech lined up to collect his runners up medal, he was confronted by Aaron Ramsey. What followed were the most shocking scenes ever witnessed in football. "Not so fast, Petr!"

The Czech keeper froze in his tracks, as Ramsey strode towards him purposefully.

"Or, should I say..." Aaron grabbed at Cech's helmet, and yanked it off, causing gasps all round, as Cech's "face" came off with it, it was a mask!

"JT!" the Welshman exclaimed.

The Arsenal squad stood there; open-mouthed, as they saw John Terry standing there in full Arsenal keeper kit.

"I knew something wasn't right the moment Petr Cech consoled me after the Brighton game" Ramsey explained, "as my head rested on his chest, it didn't feel like Petr, he felt a bit too... racist... to be Petr" he went on.

"My suspicions were confirmed after reading the interview with what was supposedly Petr Cech a few days ago. What better way to hide his true identity than to try and convince Arsenal fans that he shouldn't start the final?"

"Yeah, and I would have gotten away with it if it hadn't been for you pesky kids!"

Nah, I'm still not satisfied, let's do the Mega Happy Ending.

The Mega Happy Ending
Keep the Faith

The mega happy ending (I'm still referencing Wayne's World here, I've not suddenly turned into a twat), has taken on an even happier twist with my decision to delay it for a few days. Yes, my friends, I can confirm that The Bad Thing has not happened, and all is back to normal in the world. Okay, we might have to suffer a few months of hearing Gerry and The Pacemakers at every turn, but the alternative would have been way worse, and we can at least cancel our one-way flights to Fuckingkillmenowville and keep our social media accounts open.

More importantly; maybe, just MAYBE, we can at least try to regroup without that lot in our earholes throughout the summer.

Maybe we can write this season off, as we were prepared to do in the first place and see where the future takes us.

That would have been nigh-on impossible in the shadow of The Bad Thing. That's not all, though. There is way more to the mega happy ending than that for me. This time last year I cared about football less than I can ever remember.

You already know that this season was about me trying to rekindle my love for the game, but the longer those nine months went on - especially looking back over that time now - I've discovered it was about more than that.

Towards the end of this season, Arsenal results were pissing me off.

If I'm in a place in my life where I can be sufficiently pissed off about the result of a football match for at least 24 hours, then, for me, life is good.

It's kind of hard to explain, but I suspect that a few of you will know where I'm coming from.

Way back at the beginning of this nine-month journey which began on a sunbed in Tunisia, I mentioned that I was about to return to work after spending four months off with depression and anxiety, and this has been more than just a diary of the roller coaster ride of the football season. It's also been a journey through nine months of my life.

During that time, I have gotten a new job, and I've written this book, which the good people at Legends Publishing have been kind enough to agree to publish. (Obviously, you'd not be reading it otherwise.) Life is good.

The journey goes beyond that, however, and began four months prior to the beginning of this season, with a trip to my GP.

All of this has shown me how much supporting a football club can mirror real life. I'm not saying that you can't separate the two (you have to, or you will end up fucking insane, let alone depressed and anxious), it's more about recognising the similarities.

There are many blips along the way, and sometimes you question why you bother at all.

You enjoy the highs while you can, and the more you go through the lows, the more you appreciate the highs.

Ultimately, it's belief and blind faith that will keep you coming back for more. I'm not talking about some higher power here, because the greatest and truest faith you can have is faith in yourself. I'll leave those analogies there for now, because it's beginning to look like a song that wouldn't even make an S Club 7 reunion album (they broke up, right?)

It's been quite a ride, and I don't want to ruin it for the inevitable few of you that have read this bit before the rest of it (you know who you are, get yourself back to page one and we'll never speak of it again, yeah.)

Anyway, to sum up where I'm at right now.

I love and hate the football club I support in equal measure; I hate them for what they put me through, and I love them for the feeling like no other that they can give me.

I am in a better place in my life and with myself than I can ever remember, and sometimes I wake up in such a good mood that I irritate myself.

Football is football, and life is beautiful. Just the way things should be, and just the way I hoped this journey would end up.

Thank you for joining me on that journey, it's been quite a ride.

Who knows, I may decide to embark on the next stage of the journey in a couple of months' time on a sunbed somewhere.

Until then; Keep the Faith.

THE END... ALMOST!

EPILOGUE... LIFE IS A ROLL- ERCOASTER, JUST GOTTA RIDE IT

I f there was one thing I wanted to capture in this book, it was the rollercoaster ride of emotions that we go through during the football season.

Having read back through the whole thing, a fortnight after Arsenal's season ended with that disastrous night in Baku, I would like to think I've done just that.

I had no idea back in August exactly what was going to occur through the season, none of us ever really do, which is part of the thrill.

I mentioned during the introduction that there was always going to be the chance that this ended up a "nothing" season in terms of success but in some ways, that's actually worked out better for the purpose of this book!

This was actually the season when those emotional ups and downs returned, and I got back on that rollercoaster after spending a few years going around in circles on the Teacup ride.

I started with low expectations, but with the sense of excitement that comes with every new season heightened by the beginning of a new era.

A twenty-two-game unbeaten run had my expectations flying high, but a league season that finished, ultimately, in disappointment brought me back down to earth with a bang.

Throw the Europa League into the mix, with the euphoria of the semi-final followed a few weeks later by a crushing defeat in the final, and that's the rollercoaster life as an Arsenal fan summed up.

This was always about more than the football itself, however. This was about the reactions and the mood among the fans throughout this ride.

Personally, I've gone from liking the manager and being prepared to give him time, to questioning him while still being prepared to give him time, to being convinced that he is not the man to take us forward, all in the space of nine months.

I must admit that reading back over everything, there was more than one occasion where I thought to myself; "I can't believe I said that" and even "did I actually say that?"

There was no way I would even contemplate changing anything, though, as it would defeat the whole purpose!

Now the season is over, and I've had a bit of time to reflect, I'm in a place where I've accepted that Emery is going to be here next season, thus I am once again being prepared to give him time.

Why? Well, because if there is one thing I have learned over the past year, it's that there is no point whatsoever worrying over things that you can't control, and that the only way that life moves is forward.

The football season is over, it's time to put that one behind us.

Summer is here (it must be, it's raining as I write this), and there is so much more to enjoy out there in the real world until August, when we do this all again.

There is, of course, the madness that is the transfer window to keep you occupied if you are that way inclined but be warned; may contain Clickbait.

Acknowledgements

It's been a lifetime's ambition of mine to have a book published, and it is one that I couldn't possibly have fulfilled without the help, support and advice of so many. A heartfelt thank you...

To Dave Lane at Legends Publishing for taking a chance on me and making this whole thing possible, and not just a really long Word document growing dust in my Dropbox.

To Dave Seager for giving me the opportunity to bring my ramblings to the masses on Gunners Town in the first place, and his continuing encouragement and support for my writing. Thanks to Paul and everyone else involved in Gunners Town too.

To Andy Kelly and Mark Andrews for their help, advice, support, and for convincing me to get my arse in gear, take the plunge, and get this thing written.

Same goes to Dan Betts for taking the time to give me some early feedback and encouragement.

To Davy Boyd – the fastest retweeter in Norn Iron - for his constant support over the years, and the same goes for Gav, who does his best to keep up with Davy in the retweeting stakes.

Special thanks also go out to Glen, Coops & Steve (the other 'Spanglers!) Livers, Felmo, Nero, Kal & Den. Quiggers (I still owe you breakfast!) JBV (I told you that you'd get a mention, sunshine!)

To my friends - there are way too many of you to mention that have helped me out in one way or another, and I'm not going to make a list for fear of leaving anyone out.

I may not have mentioned everyone by name, but you know who you are, and please know that I am grateful to each and every one of you.

To my mum, dad and brother for their never-ending support, love and understanding.

To the kids - Lauren, Leah and Harry for being the reason I get up in the morning in the first place. (Hey, Lauren, I told you that Dad would write a book one day!)

Natalie, my wife, my soulmate, my best friend. Thank you for always being there for me, for standing by me, for everything you do, and everything you are.

THE END, END!